COLLECTIONS

A Harcourt Reading / Language Arts Program

*Hidden surprises are
waiting for you.
What could they be?*

COLLECTIONS

A Harcourt Reading / Language Arts Program

HIDDEN SURPRISES

SENIOR AUTHORS

Roger C. Farr • Dorothy S. Strickland • Isabel L. Beck

AUTHORS

Richard F. Abrahamson • Alma Flor Ada • Bernice E. Cullinan • Margaret McKeown • Nancy Roser
Patricia Smith • Judy Wallis • Junko Yokota • Hallie Kay Yopp

SENIOR CONSULTANT

Asa G. Hilliard III

CONSULTANTS

Karen S. Kutiper • David A. Monti • Angelina Olivares

Harcourt

Orlando   Boston   Dallas   Chicago   San Diego

Visit *The Learning Site!*

www.harcourtschool.com

Dear Reader,

Opening a new book is like opening the door to a new world. When you read books, you can visit new places, learn new facts, and make new friends. The things you learn can be surprising!

As you read **Hidden Surprises**, you will meet characters who learn about themselves and others. You may discover animals you have never seen before. You may even see some old friends in new stories.

Reading is the key to the world of **Hidden Surprises**. You will learn things this year that will help you become a better reader. As your reading skills grow, you will open the door to more wonderful surprises in the future.

Come along! Discover the hidden surprises that are waiting for you.

Sincerely,

The Authors

The Authors

SOMETHING SPECIAL!

CONTENTS

3

What a Team!

Seven True Dog Stories
by MARGARET DAVIDSON
Pictures by SUSANNE SUBA

OFFICER BUCKLE AND GLORIA

SAVIOUR PIROTTA · NILESH MISTRY
Turtle Bay

Ranger Rick
National Wildlife Federation
August 1996

Little Grunt and the Big Egg
A Prehistoric Fairy Tale
Tomie dePaola

4

CONTENTS

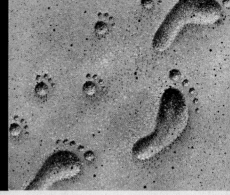

CONTENTS

THEME
Friends Grow

to
With

7

Using Reading Strategies

A strategy is a plan for doing something well.

You probably already use some strategies as you read. For example, you may **look at the title and pictures before you begin reading** a story. You may **think about what you want to find out while reading.** Using strategies like these can help you become a better reader.

Look at the list of strategies on page 9. You will learn about and use these strategies as you read the selections in this book. As you read, look back at the list to remind yourself of the **strategies good readers use.**

- Use Prior Knowledge
- Make and Confirm Predictions
- Adjust Reading Rate
- Self-Question
- Create Mental Images
- Use Context to Confirm Meaning
- Use Text Structure and Format
- Use Graphic Aids
- Use Reference Sources
- Read Ahead
- Reread
- Summarize

Here are some ways to check your own comprehension:

✔ Make a copy of this list on a piece of construction paper shaped like a bookmark.

✔ Have it handy as you read.

✔ After reading, talk with a classmate about which strategies you used and why.

SOMETHING SPECIAL!

CONTENTS

READER'S

Frida María
by Deborah Nourse Lattimore

HISTORICAL FICTION

Frida María finds she cannot please everyone, but at the fiesta, she proves she is something special!

Award-Winning Author and Illustrator

READER'S CHOICE LIBRARY

Julian's Glorious Summer
by Ann Cameron

REALISTIC FICTION

Find out why Julian is downright unhappy when his friend Gloria gets a new bike.

Award-Winning Author

READER'S CHOICE LIBRARY

CHOICE

The Treasure Hunt

by Bill Cosby

REALISTIC FICTION

Everyone else in his family has a hobby or a talent, so Little Bill sets out to find what makes him special.

Notable Trade Book in Social Studies

The Math Wiz

by Betsy Duffey

REALISTIC FICTION/ NOVEL

Marty discovers that his excellent math skills can help him win friends.

Award-Winning Author and Illustrator

Appelemando's Dreams

by Patricia Polacco

FANTASY

Appelemando has dreams that he and his friends can see! His dreams get him first into trouble and then out of it.

Award-Winning Author and Illustrator

ARTHUR
WRITES A STORY

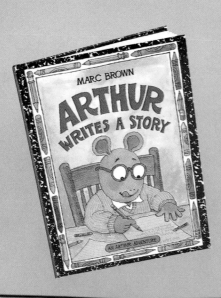

Children's
Choice

MARC BROWN

Arthur's teacher, Mr. Ratburn, explained the homework.
"What should the story be about?" Arthur asked.
"Anything," Mr. Ratburn said. "Write about something
that is important to you."

Arthur started his story the minute he got home.
He knew exactly what he wanted to write about.

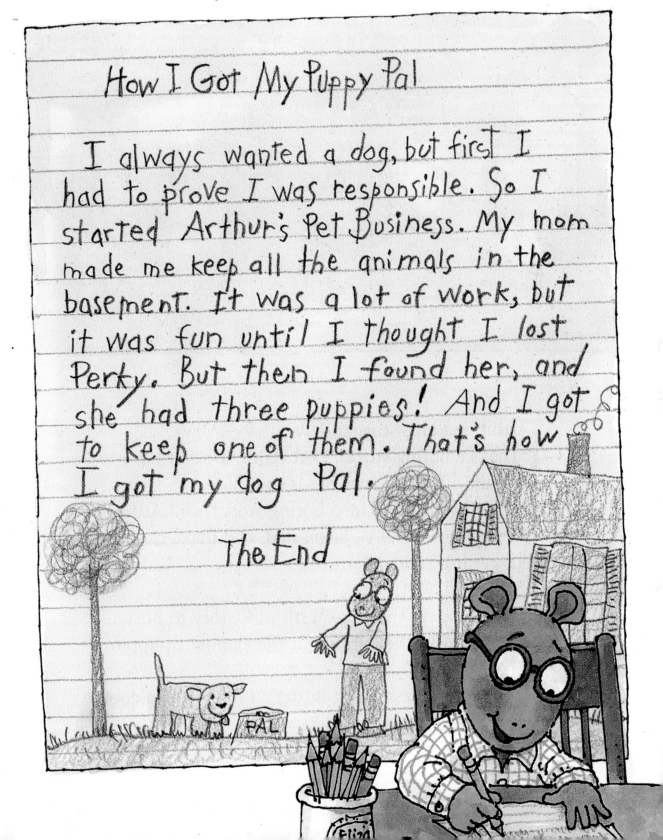

How I Got My Puppy Pal

I always wanted a dog, but first I
had to prove I was responsible. So I
started Arthur's Pet Business. My mom
made me keep all the animals in the
basement. It was a lot of work, but
it was fun until I thought I lost
Perky. But then I found her, and
she had three puppies! And I got
to keep one of them. That's how
I got my dog Pal.

The End

Arthur read his story to D.W.

"That's a boring story," D.W. said. "Does it have to be real life? Because your life is so dull."

"I don't want to write a boring story," said Arthur.

"If it were me," D.W. suggested, "I'd make the story about getting an elephant."

The next day, Arthur read his new story to Buster.

"Did you like the part about the elephant puppies?" he asked.

"It's okay, I guess," said Buster. "I'm writing a cool story about outer space."

Maybe my story should take place on the moon, thought Arthur.

On Wednesday, Arthur read his newest story to the Brain.

"Scientifically speaking, elephants would weigh less on the moon, but wouldn't float that high," said the Brain.

"So you don't like it?" asked Arthur.

"A good story should be well researched," said the Brain. "Like mine: 'If I Had a Pet Stegosaurus in the Jurassic Period.'"

Arthur hurried to the library.

"What are all those books for?" asked Francine.

"Research," said Arthur. "I'm writing about my pet five-toed mammal of the genus *Loxodonta*."

"Your *what*?" asked Francine.

"My elephant!" Arthur explained.

"Oh," said Francine. "I'm putting jokes in my story."

All through dinner, Arthur worried about his story.
"Please pass the corn," asked Father.
"Corn! That's it!" said Arthur. "Purple corn and blue
elephants! On Planet Shmellafint! Now *that's* funny."
"Arthur is acting weirder than usual," said D.W.

On Thursday, everyone at the Sugar Bowl was talking about their stories.

"Last year, a kid wrote a country-western song for her story," said Prunella. "And she got an A+."

"How do you know?" asked Arthur.

"That kid was me," explained Prunella. "Mr. Ratburn said I should send it to a record company. It was *that* good."

"Wow!" said Arthur.

That night, Arthur's imagination went wild.
He decided to turn his story into a song. He
even made up a dance to go with it.

26

Later, he tried it out on his family.
". . . Now this little boy
Can go home and enjoy
His own personal striped elephant.
And you will see
How happy he will be
Here on Planet . . . Shmellafint!"

"Well," said Arthur. "What do you think?"

Mother and Father smiled.
"It's nice," said Grandma Thora. "But a little confusing."
"Too bad you can't dance," said D.W.
"What am I going to do?" said Arthur. "My story is due tomorrow."
That night Arthur didn't sleep very well.

The next day, Arthur worried until Mr. Ratburn finally called on him.

When Arthur's song and dance was over, the classroom was so quiet, it was almost spooky. Binky raised his hand. "Did that really happen?"

"Sort of," said Arthur. "It started as the story of how I got my dog."

"I'd like to hear that story," said Mr. Ratburn.

"The title was 'How I Got My Puppy Pal,'" said Arthur.

Arthur told how proud he was of his pet business and how scared he was when Perky disappeared. And he told how happy he was to find her under his bed and how surprised he was to see her three puppies.

"And the best part is," said Arthur, "I got to keep one!"

Buster said, "I like that story better than your other one."

"Great story!" said Binky.

"I think Arthur's story was the best!" said Francine.

"Good work," said Mr. Ratburn. "Of course, I expect you to write it all down by Monday."

Then Mr. Ratburn gave Arthur a gold sticker. "Oh, and one more thing," he said.

"Leave out the dancing!"

THINK ABOUT IT

1 How does Arthur find out he is good at writing stories about real life?

2 What part of "Arthur Writes a Story" did you like the best? Why?

3 How can you tell that Arthur's first story is about real life and his second story is made up?

MEET THE AUTHOR
MARC

Marc Brown is well-known as the author and illustrator of more than twenty *Arthur* books. He first made up Arthur while he was telling his son a bedtime story. Marc Brown enjoys telling stories and, most of all, drawing pictures for stories.

AND ILLUSTRATOR
BROWN

Marc Brown did not have many books when he was a boy. His Grandma Thora used to tell him and his sisters stories that she made up. Marc loved her stories!

When his first son, Tolon, was born, Marc Brown started telling him stories, just as Grandma Thora had done. He found that he enjoyed this, and Tolon enjoyed it, too. Marc Brown decided to write books for children, and that is how the *Arthur* books began!

Here are more Arthur *stories.*
Have you read them yet?

 Visit *The Learning Site!*
www.harcourtschool.com

RESPONSE

WRITE A STORY

Arthur writes a story about how he got his puppy, Pal. Write a story about how you got one of your favorite things. Remember that your story needs a beginning, a middle, and an end. Share your story with some classmates.

BE A WRITING COACH

ROLE-PLAY

Arthur gets ideas for his new stories from his sister and his friends. If you were one of Arthur's friends, what ideas would you give him? Role-play a scene with a classmate in which you give Arthur some tips for writing his story.

ACTIVITIES

COVER STORY

MAKE A BOOK COVER

In one of his stories, Arthur puts blue elephants and purple corn on a planet he names Shmellafint. Think of an idea for another story that takes place on a planet with a funny name. Make a book cover for this story. Draw a picture of the planet and some characters. Make up a title, too.

MAKE US LAUGH

TELL A JOKE

Francine told Arthur she was using jokes in her story. Find a book of silly jokes and pick a few that you like. Practice telling these jokes. Remember to speak clearly. Then share the jokes with your classmates.

Prefixes and Suffixes

In "Arthur Writes a Story," Arthur tells how he got his puppy. He could have written these sentences to tell what happened.

> Perky **appeared** with three puppies! I was scared when I thought she had **disappeared.**

Look at the word *disappeared*. What letters have been added to *appeared*?

dis- **+** appeared **=** disappeared

A word part added to the beginning of a word is a **prefix.** When a prefix is added to a base word, the meaning of the word changes. A word part added to the end of a word is a **suffix.** Adding a suffix changes the way a word is used.

Prefix and Its Meaning	Base Word	Suffix	New Word
dis- ("not")	agree		disagree
non- ("not")	fiction		nonfiction
over- ("over")	head		overhead
	wash	-able	washable
	introduce	-tion, -ion	introduction

Knowing the parts of a word can help you figure out its meaning. Read the note below. What do the underlined words mean? Use the chart on page 38 to help you.

Dear Arthur,

I <u>disagree</u> with the Brain. I liked your <u>nonsense</u> story about elephants on the moon. Why don't you have an elephant take an <u>overland</u> trip in a Moon Rover? That could be a very funny and <u>enjoyable</u> story.

Your friend,
Francine

WHAT HAVE YOU LEARNED?

1. If someone says a person is likable, what does he or she mean? How does the suffix help you?

2. What does this sign mean?

 Visit *The Learning Site!*
www.harcourtschool.com

TRY THIS • TRY THIS • TRY THIS

Add a prefix or a suffix from the first box below to one of the words in the second box. Then write a sentence with each new word you make.

Prefixes and Suffixes
dis-
-able
-ion

Base Words
drink
direct
honest

Marta's Magnets

by Wendy Pfeffer
illustrated by Gail Piazza

Marta loved to collect things. She collected sticks
and stones, cards and cardboard, little boxes, big boxes,
and . . . well, just about anything. So, when Marta's
family moved, her collections moved, too . . . right into
the room Marta shared with her older sister, Rosa.

41

Rosa's side of the room was sparkling clean.
Marta's wasn't. Her bed was covered with crepe
paper from broken-open piñatas. Her mirror was
hidden by chains made from gum wrappers. On
her desk sat a ball of string, the size of a soccer ball,
and a shoe box full of magnets.

Colleen, Rosa's new friend who lived across the hall,
peeked into the bedroom. "What a lot of junk," she said.

"Yeah!" agreed Rosa.

"My collections are not junk. They're my treasures,"
said Marta, sorting through her magnets, trying to
ignore Rosa and Colleen.

Marta found the bar magnets from a birthday grab bag. She saw the magnets she'd cut from the bottom of an old shower curtain. And she picked up the horseshoe magnet that she had saved from an old science kit. But Marta's favorite was the truck-shaped magnet a pizza delivery boy had given her. She stuck it in her pocket.

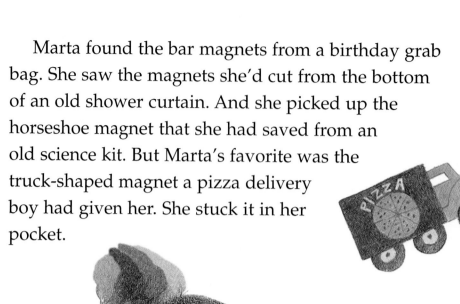

In the kitchen Marta poured herself some juice from the refrigerator. As she drank, she kept sticking her truck magnet on the door and peeling it off.

"More junk, Marta?" said Rosa, sharing her sunflower seeds with Colleen.

"I don't call your bottles of nail polish and glitter junk," Marta said, angrily stomping into her room.

She looked outside over a city of tar roofs. It looked like one huge parking lot.

Five floors down a bunch of kids were playing in the street. Marta had walked past them that morning. But they didn't speak to her. Two boys were kicking a can. Three girls were jumping rope. Marta listened to the girls' singsong raplike chant.

"One potato, two potato, three potato, four.
Jump to the window. Jump to the door.
Five potato, six potato, seven potato, eight.
Jump to the garden. Jump to the gate."

Grabbing her magnets, Marta bounced down five flights of stairs and ran out the door. "Hey, guys!" she called. "My name's Marta."

The boys kept kicking the can. The girls kept jumping rope.

Marta stuck one of her magnets on an iron railing, another on a fire hydrant, and a third on a traffic sign.

The kids stopped playing. "What're you doing?" asked the taller boy.

"Sticking magnets on things," said Marta. "This truck stuck on my refrigerator door. Want to try a magnet?" she added, offering one to each kid.

"Sure," said the tall boy, "I'm Marshall."

"My name's Stevie," said the other boy. "Over there is Kim. She doesn't talk much."

Kim peeked over her glasses. She rubbed the smooth edges of the magnet Marta handed her and smiled.

One of the girls put down her ends of the rope. "My name's Tanya, and this is Vanya," she said. "We're twins."

Vanya stuck her magnet in her pocket. "Want to jump rope?" she asked.

"Sure!" said Marta, as Tanya began to chant,

> "One potato, two potato, three potato, four.
>   A truck got stuck on Marta's door.
> Five potato, six potato, seven potato, eight.
>   Maybe it'll stick on the garden gate."

Marta joined in. She loved the slip-slap, slip-slap rhythm of the rope skipping on the sidewalk. She jumped until Stevie yelled, "This horseshoe stuck to the air conditioner."

Marshall waved his magnet. "Magnets attract a lot of things. See, mine sticks to this old steel can."

In a few minutes excited voices seemed to drift up and bounce off the brick row houses.

"This magnet doesn't stick to my soda can."

"Hey, the magnet stuck to the key in my pocket."

"Mine doesn't stick to my key."

"This one sticks to the nail in the door, but not the door."

Then a voice, like a whisper, floated among the others.

"This magnet doesn't stick to my glasses," said Kim.

Marta smiled. Her magnets were special — they attracted friends, and they made Kim speak.

Marta turned toward Rosa and Colleen. She hoped they saw her five new friends. But Rosa was on her hands and knees, and Colleen was crying. Marta ran over to them.

"Colleen lost her key ring down this grating," said Rosa. "She can't get into her apartment without her key. She can't take the stew out of the freezer. Dinner won't be on time. Her mom will be late for night school. And . . ."

"I have an idea," said Marta. She ran into her building and climbed the stairs.

The smell of chicken soup drifted over the first floor. Bright colors decorated the second floor walls. Bicycles and hockey sticks filled the third floor hall. A baby crying told Marta she must be on the fourth floor. And the fifth floor smelled like home. An apartment building is a collection, too . . . of different people. Marta ran into her apartment and came out carrying her ball of string.

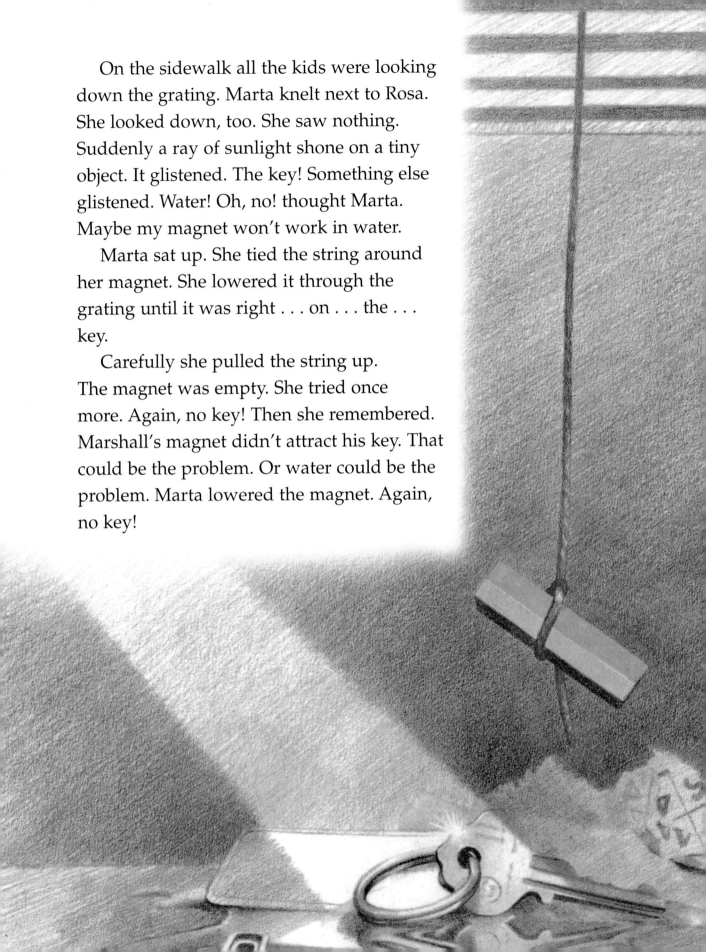

On the sidewalk all the kids were looking down the grating. Marta knelt next to Rosa. She looked down, too. She saw nothing. Suddenly a ray of sunlight shone on a tiny object. It glistened. The key! Something else glistened. Water! Oh, no! thought Marta. Maybe my magnet won't work in water.

Marta sat up. She tied the string around her magnet. She lowered it through the grating until it was right . . . on . . . the . . . key.

Carefully she pulled the string up. The magnet was empty. She tried once more. Again, no key! Then she remembered. Marshall's magnet didn't attract his key. That could be the problem. Or water could be the problem. Marta lowered the magnet. Again, no key!

The next time she lowered the magnet she aimed at the
key ring. But that was in the water, too. The magnet swayed
back and forth over the key ring. Suddenly — Wham! — they
connected. Inch by inch she pulled the string up.

"There's the key ring," yelled Rosa. "It's dangling from
the magnet."

"So are four paper clips," Marta said. "My magnet is a collector, too."

Colleen grabbed the key ring and gave Marta a big hug. "Hooray for Marta's magnet!" the kids yelled.

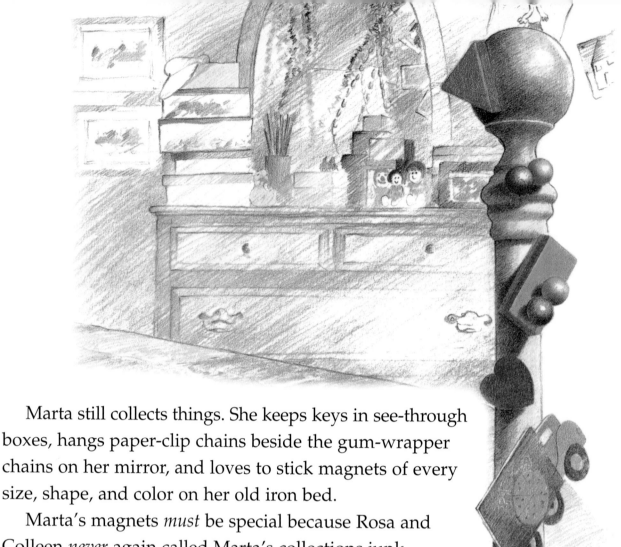

Marta still collects things. She keeps keys in see-through boxes, hangs paper-clip chains beside the gum-wrapper chains on her mirror, and loves to stick magnets of every size, shape, and color on her old iron bed.

Marta's magnets *must* be special because Rosa and Colleen *never* again called Marta's collections junk.

Think About It

1 How do Marta's magnets help her make friends?

2 What is your favorite part of the story? Why do you like that part?

3 How would you describe Marta? What clues does the author give that help you get to know Marta?

Meet the Author

Wendy Pfeffer

No one in Wendy Pfeffer's family was a writer, but she knew at a very young age that she wanted to write. Her father loved to learn about words and where they come from. Her grandfather spent hours telling stories to his grandchildren. Growing up in this family, Wendy learned to love reading and acting out stories.

When Wendy was very young, she started writing retellings of stories she knew, such as "Hansel and Gretel." Later, she wrote in her diary, and in high school she worked on the school newspaper.

As an adult, Wendy Pfeffer became a teacher and even opened a new school. Although she no longer teaches, Wendy Pfeffer still works with children and enjoys writing for them.

Visit *The Learning Site!*
www.harcourtschool.com

WORKING WITH MAGNETS

Magnets can pull metal objects or push them away. Magnets are very useful to us every day. Can you think of places you have seen them? You can learn more about magnets in these activities.

High Flier

How far does a magnet's power reach? A magnet can hold something in the air without even touching it. See how a magnet's power, or "magnetism," reaches out and pulls an object toward it.

You will need:

Paper

Strong bar magnet

Tape

Paper clip

Thread

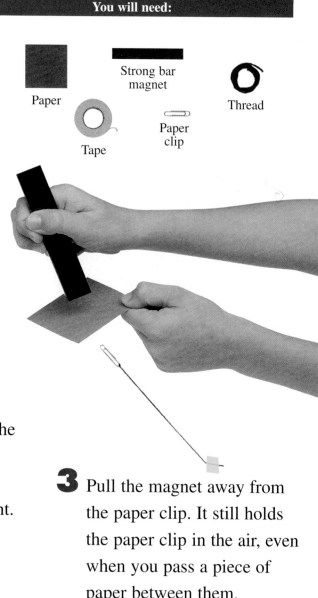

1 Tie the thread to the paper clip. Knot it tightly. Tape the other end to a table top.

2 Use the magnet to pick up the paper clip. Lift the magnet until the thread is straight.

3 Pull the magnet away from the paper clip. It still holds the paper clip in the air, even when you pass a piece of paper between them.

Pair of Poles

The two ends, or "poles," of a magnet have different names. One is the north pole and the other is the south pole. Learn how to find out which is which.

You will need:

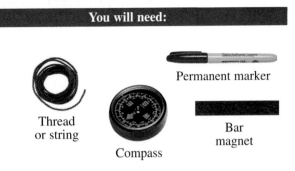

Thread or string

Compass

Permanent marker

Bar magnet

1 A compass needle is a magnet with its north pole at its tip. Therefore, it always points north. Use a compass to find north.

2 Tie the thread around the center of the bar magnet so that it balances.

3 Hold the magnet up by the string, and let it settle. Keep the magnet a few feet away from the compass.

The magnet's south pole points south.

The magnet's north pole points north.

4 Mark the end pointing south with a marker.

Think About It

What have you learned about magnets?

Response

Making Connections
MAKE A CHART
Marta's magnet picks up Colleen's key ring, but it cannot pick up the key. The magnet attracts the key ring but does not attract the key. Use a magnet in the classroom. Find objects the magnet will attract and objects it will not attract. Make a chart that shows what you learned about magnets in this experiment and in the selection "Working with Magnets."

Fun and Games
MAKE UP A SONG
With two or three classmates, create a song that you might sing while jumping rope or playing a game. You may use a tune you already know. Add actions and share your song with classmates.

Activities

Hello! What's Your Name?
WRITE A LIST

Moving to a new place is not always easy. Think about how Marta makes friends in her new neighborhood. How could you welcome a new classmate or neighbor? Write a list of ideas for ways to make new friends.

We Are All Special
WRITE A POEM

We all have something that we can do well. Write a poem that describes you and one other person. Tell how each of you is special.

RONALD MORGAN
GOES TO CAMP

BY PATRICIA REILLY GIFF

ILLUSTRATED BY SUSANNA NATTI

It was summer. School was over.

"Bad news," I said. "There's nothing to do."

"Good news, Ronald Morgan," said Michael. "We can go to camp."

Ronald Morgan Goes to Camp
by Patricia Reilly Giff

illustrated by Susanna Natti

"Good," said Jan.

"Great," said Rosemary. "Maybe we can win some medals."

"Yes," said Michael. "You just have to be good at something."

I thought for a minute. I wasn't good at anything. "I don't think I'll go," I said.

But Billy shook his head. "Then you'll really have nothing to do."

Billy was right. My father brought up my suitcase, and my mother sewed on name tags. At the last minute, I filled my pockets with my old green sunglasses, the harmonica Aunt Ruth gave me, two plaid Band-Aids just in case, a cracker, and a box of raisins that I found under my socks.

Everyone came to the station,
even Lucky.

My father yelled, "Good-bye!"
My mother threw a kiss. And
Aunt Ruth called, "Don't forget
to write."

"Uh oh," I said, "I think
I forgot to pack a pencil."

Inside the bus we sang:

Friends we make
at Camp Echo Lake . . .

But Rosemary didn't sing. "I'm going to win a pile of medals," she was telling the bus driver. "For swimming, and diving, and running, and . . ."

I didn't sing either. I was trying to think of something I was good at.

And Jan didn't sing. "I always get sick on the bus," she said. I reached into my pocket. I gave her some raisins.

"Try these," I said. "Maybe you'll feel better."

"They have dust on them," she said.

"But they're really good."

Then Jimmy yelled, "Hey! We're here! It's Camp Echo Lake."

Ms. Conrad, our counselor, was waiting. "Call me Connie," she said. She walked us back and forth to see the lake, the hill, and the pine trees.

"Look," said Michael. We slid down to watch a green frog, and then a duck with a bunch of brown feathers, who was quacking at us.

"What a great swimmer," Michael said. I broke up a cracker for the duck.

"Do you think I'm good at anything?" I asked.

Michael raised his shoulders in the air. "Sure," he said. "I guess so."

We quacked as we ran to catch up with everyone. Tom was saying, "I think that's a poisonous bug."

I looked closer. "I think it's only a daddy-long-legs."

On Tuesday, we had bug juice and bananas for a snack. Jan had another raisin, too. Then I sat up on Lookout Rock and practiced my song. In out, in out . . . on the harmonica. It *almost* sounded like

Friends we make
at Camp Echo Lake . . .

"Look out, rock!" Michael yelled. "I'm climbing up." But he slipped.

I dived to catch him, and we rolled down the hill together. It was kind of fun.

And then it was time to swim. Maybe I was good at that.
Connie called out, "Ready . . . set . . . jump!"

Rosemary was the first one in. "Look," she said. "A little
snake."

And I said, "I think I'll call him Snakey."

But Tom yelled, "That snake is after me!"

I took giant steps across the rocks to pull him out, but I
splashed into the water.

"Quack," said Michael.

"Quack," I said back.

On Wednesday, Connie said, "It's time for hide-and-seek."

Billy counted: "Two four six . . ." Michael ran one way, Jan ran the other. "Raisins make me go fast," she called back.

Tom and I crashed through the bushes.

"Hey," Tom said, "we're lost in a mosquito nest." I played my harmonica as loud as I could, so someone could find us.

"You're IT, Ronald Morgan," Billy said. But first I pulled out the Band-Aids to cover the bites. One for Tom and one for me.

Thursday night was camp-out. I wore my sweats with the muddy knees. At the campfire, we toasted marshmallows on sticks. We told stories, too.

Michael told about a dog, and Alice told about a GREAT GRAY SCARY—

"Stop!" said Jan, with her hands over her ears.

I'm not so good at stories, so instead I played my harmonica, and everyone sang:

Friends we make
at Camp Echo Lake . . .

On Friday, we made *I Missed You* cards for our mothers and fathers. I drew one for Lucky, too.

"Nice work," Connie told everyone.

But Jimmy said, "I *really* miss my mother. I miss my TV, too."

"Wait," I said. I lent him my old green sunglasses so no one would know his eyes were red.

And then it was Saturday.
Medal Day. First we drew pictures.
Then we stuck tiny stones on the
paper with glue.

"Work hard," said Connie. "We'll show them to everyone."

We spent a long time looking for stones. Then we rushed
to clean and pack and make lemonade, because people were
coming up the drive. My mother and father, Aunt Ruth, and
even Lucky in a picnic basket.

"It's medal time," said Connie. "Everyone was good at something."

I shook my head. "Not me."

Rosemary's medal was for swimming, and Jan's was for running. Billy's was for hide-and-seek, and Michael's was for telling stories.

At last it was my turn. "Ronald . . ." said Connie. I held my breath. "You get a medal for . . . being a good friend."

"She's right," said Michael.

"Yes," said Jan. And everybody cheered.

Then I played the harmonica one last time, while everybody sang:

Friends we make
At Camp Echo Lake . . .

THINK ABOUT IT

1 How does Ronald show that he is a good friend?

2 How do the things that Ronald takes to camp turn out to be important?

3 Do you think Ronald is happy that he decided to go to camp? Tell why you think as you do.

Meet the Author
PATRICIA REILLY GIFF

Patricia Reilly Giff loves to read. This is why she became a writer. When she was younger, she read all the time. Her sister had to take books out of Patricia's hands to get her attention.

Patricia Reilly Giff likes to write about things in her life. She also writes about people she knows. She was a teacher for twenty years. Many of her characters are like some students she knew. The character of Ronald Morgan is just like a helpful boy she had in one of her classes.

Patricia Reilly Giff likes to write books that show how people are special. She says she became a writer "to say to all the children I've loved that they are special, . . . that all of us are special and important just because we are ourselves."

Meet the Illustrator
SUSANNA NATTI

Susanna Natti knew she wanted to be an artist when she was a young girl. She grew up in Massachusetts around many writers and artists. Her own mother wrote books for children, and Susanna knew she wanted to work on children's books, too.

Before she went to art school, Susanna Natti took lessons from a family friend. He showed her how to draw people and animals and how to make her drawings seem to move. She still draws the way that friend taught her to years ago. First she does a quick sketch, and then she goes back and finishes the picture.

Susanna Natti lives in her home state of Massachusetts, with her husband and two daughters.

Visit *The Learning Site!*
www.harcourtschool.com

SUSANNA NATTI

Response

WRITE A LETTER

Imagine you are away at camp. Write a letter to a family member or a friend, telling what camp is like. You might tell how you felt when you first got there and whether your feelings have now changed. Write about something interesting or funny that has happened.

Snakes Alive

MAKE A POSTER

Ronald Morgan was not afraid of the snake in the water because he knew it was not harmful. Can you tell the difference between a dangerous snake and one that is not dangerous? In the library, look for information about the snakes that live in your state. Make a poster showing some of the ones to watch out for.

Activities

The Medal Goes To . . .

PRESENT AN AWARD

Ronald Morgan was given a medal for being a good friend. Think of someone you know who is good at something. Make up an award for that person, and share it with your classmates. Tell why the person should get the award.

Pack Your Suitcase

REMEMBER A LIST

Imagine you are going away to camp. With a group of classmates, play a memory game. The first person says, "I am going to camp. In my suitcase I will pack . . ." The next person must then repeat what was said and add something else. How long can you remember everything on the list?

Predict Outcomes

When you read "Ronald Morgan Goes to Camp," did you think about what might happen next? Thinking about what might happen is called **making predictions.** Making predictions can help you be a better reader. It can also make reading more fun!

When you make predictions, you are like a detective. You use **clues** in the story to help you predict. You also use what you already know. A drawing like this can help you make predictions.

Clue in the Story
Ronald Morgan wants to win a medal.

What I Know
Characters in stories often solve their problems.

Prediction
Ronald Morgan will win a medal.

Sometimes you find new clues as you read on. This means you are being an **active reader** and a good detective. Think about the new clues and about what you already know. Then make new predictions.

Keep looking for more clues as you read on. You might even change your predictions again!

Read the paragraphs below. What might happen next?

"Dad! I heard a noise!" whispered Joey, as Kelly shook their father's sleeping bag. "There's something outside!"

"I left my shoes outside, Dad," said Kelly. "What if a bear takes them?"

Dad was awake now. "There are no bears around here. It's probably something much smaller. Did you leave anything else out there?" he said.

"Only the cooler," said Joey, "but we put it up on the picnic bench."

WHAT HAVE YOU LEARNED?

1. What are the two things you use to make predictions?

2. Suppose you were reading a story about a person who was very, very happy. What kinds of things would you predict that person might do? Why?

Visit *The Learning Site!*
www.harcourtschool.com

TRY THIS • TRY THIS • TRY THIS

Suppose that, in the story above, Joey heard a noise *inside* the tent. Think about how your predictions might change. Draw a web like the one on page 82 to show what information you would use to make a new prediction.

ALLIE'S Basketball

by
Barbara E. Barber

illustrated by
Darryl Ligasan

Dream

When Allie's father came home from work Friday evening, he brought her a gift. "Because I love you," he said, and kissed Allie on her nose. The gift was something that Allie really wanted—a basketball.

The next day, Allie and her father walked to the playground. Allie loved the sound her new basketball made as she bounced it on the sidewalk. As they passed the firehouse, they waved to Mr. Puchinsky, the fire captain.

"Hi, Domino!" Allie called to the firehouse dog. Domino wagged his tail and licked Allie's basketball when she held it for him to sniff.

At the playground, Allie scanned the basketball courts while her father talked with Mr. Gonzalez, the park monitor. Some older kids already had a game going. All of the players were boys. They hardly ever missed a shot.

"Go ahead and practice, and then we'll shoot baskets together as soon as I get back from taking Aunt Harriet shopping," Allie's father told her. "I'll just be across the street. If you need me, tell Mr. Gonzalez, and he'll come get me."

"Okay," Allie replied.

89

She waved good-bye and ran to an empty court.
She lifted her new basketball over her head and aimed.
The shot missed. She aimed again. She missed again.

One of the boys playing in the next court noticed
Allie and started to laugh. The others joined in.

"*Boys,*" Allie mumbled. Then she dribbled and
bounced. And bounced and dribbled.

Allie's friend Keisha came into the playground
with her hula hoop. Keisha saw Allie and held the
hoop up. Allie aimed her basketball and . . . *Zoom!*
Right through the middle.

"Let's play basketball!" Allie said.

"I don't know how," Keisha answered.

"I'll show you."

Keisha twirled her hula hoop. "My brother says basketball's a boy's game."

"Your brother doesn't know what he's talking about," Allie said.

She aimed at an empty trash can. She stepped back a few feet, and took a shot.

Thump! In!

Allie noticed her neighbor Buddy jumping rope with her friend Sheba and another girl. When he missed he ran off to join some other kids who wanted to use his volleyball.

"Hi, Allie!" Sheba called. "Is that your basketball?"

"Yep, my dad gave it to me. Want to shoot some baskets?"

"Maybe later," Sheba replied. "Want to jump double-dutch?"

"Maybe later," Allie said.

Allie pretended she was playing soccer. She kicked the ball and chased it. Then she looked up at the basket, aimed, and shot. The ball struck the backboard, then the rim, and bounded off.

Julio, who was in Allie's class at school, whizzed by on his skateboard. He made a sharp turn when he noticed the new basketball.

"Wow!" Julio exclaimed. "Is that yours?"

"Yes," said Allie proudly. "Let's shoot some baskets!"

Julio looked at Allie, his eyes wide. "You must be kidding!" he said. "Me shoot baskets with a girl? No, thanks!" He laughed and skated away.

Allie heaved a sigh and eyed the basket. She took another shot. The ball circled the rim and fell off. She heard some of the boys in the next court chuckle. She tried again. And again.

Allie sighed again and plopped down on a bench. Buddy walked over, bouncing his volleyball. "What's up?" he asked. "Something wrong with your basketball?"

"Well . . ." Allie hesitated.

"I'll trade you my volleyball for it! It's smaller and lighter—it'll be easier for you to play with."

"I don't know," Allie said.

Buddy reached into his pocket. He took out a miniature sports car, two quarters, and some grape bubble gum—Allie's favorite. "You can have these *and* my volleyball for the basketball," he said.

Allie thought it over. She remembered the first time her father took her to a basketball game at Madison Square Garden. She loved it all: The noise of the crowd, the bright lights on the court, and especially the slam-dunks the players made look so easy! She knew right then and there that one day, she would be a professional basketball player, too . . .

Allie hugged her basketball close. "No way I'm getting rid of this ball! It's a gift from my dad. Someday I'm going to be the best basketball player ever!"

"Well," Buddy snorted, "some guys think girls shouldn't be playin' basketball."

"That's dumb!" Allie bounced her ball. "My cousin Gwen plays on one of the best high school teams in her state. She's won more than ten trophies!"

Buddy looked surprised.

"Some girls think boys shouldn't be jumping rope," Allie continued. "They think boys are no good at it. That's dumb, too."

Buddy unwrapped two pieces of gum. "Want some?"

Allie and Buddy blew huge purple bubbles. They popped their gum so loud that Domino ran over to investigate. He pranced right up to Allie and sniffed her basketball.

"Wanna play basketball, Domino? Come on, boy, let's play!"

Domino ran alongside Allie as she dribbled and bounced. Laughing, Allie turned toward the basket, and took a long-distance shot. The ball brushed against the backboard, rolled around the rim, and dropped in!

Buddy jumped up from the bench. "Nice shot, Allie!" he yelled, and ran to retrieve the ball.

"Thanks," Allie said, beaming.

Julio saw the shot, too. So did Sheba. They both hurried to the center of the court.

"Here!" Allie and Julio and Sheba called to Buddy almost in one voice.

Buddy dribbled the ball, then passed it to Allie. She took a shot and missed.

"Don't worry, Allie!" Buddy yelled. Julio and Sheba each shot and missed. Allie caught the ball and dribbled closer to the basket. *I can't wait to show Dad what I can do,* she thought.

Up, up went the ball. It didn't touch the backboard. It didn't touch the rim. It didn't touch anything.

Zoom! In!

The older boys in the next court applauded. Mr. Gonzalez whistled. Domino barked. Above all the noise rose a familiar voice—Allie's father.

"That-a-girl!" he shouted. "Hooray for Allie!"

Think About It

1 What does Allie learn about playing basketball?

2 What kind of person is Allie? How do you know?

3 What is Allie's dream? Do you think it can come true? Explain your answer.

MEET THE AUTHOR
Barbara E. Barber

Dear Readers,

I have always loved to write. My mother says I've been writing since the second grade. I enjoy writing poetry as well as stories. My friends and family thought I should send my writing to publishers, and so I did.

Allie's Basketball Dream is my second picture book to be published. Allie's story comes from my own childhood. I liked to play basketball, punchball, and touch football. Just like Allie, I learned that practice makes perfect.

It takes time to become good at a sport. Be patient with yourself. Remember, you can do it if you try!

Your friend,

Barbara E. Barber

MEET THE ILLUSTRATOR
Darryl Ligasan

Dear Readers,

I am an illustrator. I draw and paint pictures that help an author tell a story. For *Allie's Basketball Dream,* I tried something new. These pictures were made on a computer!

First I used a pencil to draw sketches on paper. Then I used a special tool called a scanner, which took pictures of the sketches and put them into the computer. Instead of using paints and a brush, I used the computer to add details and colors to the sketches. Did you notice that parts of some pictures seem stretched? I had the computer do that for me, too!

Your friend,

Darryl Ligasan

Visit *The Learning Site!*
www.harcourtschool.com

TO...

by LEE BENNETT HOPKINS
illustration by Mark Bender

TO

make
this world
a whole lot
brighter

when
I
grow up
I'll
be
a writer.
I'll
write about
some things
I know —

how to bunt
how to throw . . .

a Christmas wish
a butter dish . . .

a teddy bear
an empty chair . . .

the love I have inside
to
share . . .

Yes.

To
make
this world
a whole lot
brighter,

when
I grow up
I'll
be
a
writer.

105

RESPONSE

▶ **I Can Do It!**

WRITE A STORY

It takes Allie many tries before she can "shoot a basket." She feels very proud of herself. Write about a time when you were learning how to do something difficult, like riding a bicycle. Compare your feelings to Allie's. Describe how you felt when you were able to do it at last.

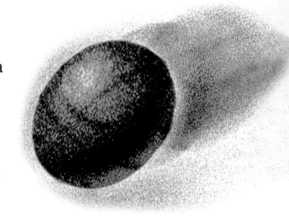

▶ **Sports News**

READ ALOUD

Listen to a television or radio reporter telling about a sports event. The reporter makes the game sound so exciting that you feel as if you are watching it. Cut out a sports report from the newspaper. Practice reading it so that it sounds exciting. Then read the report to classmates the way a sports reporter would.

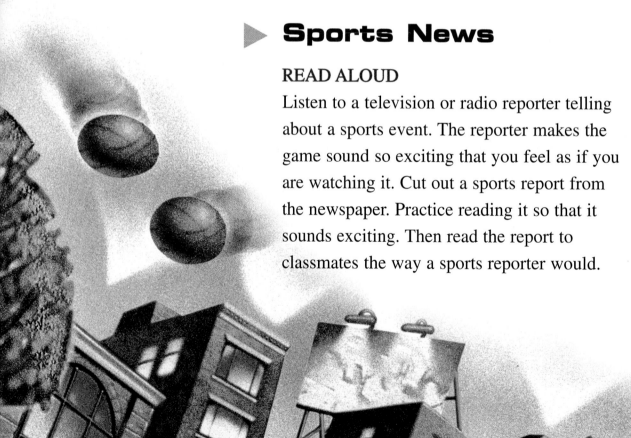

ACTIVITIES

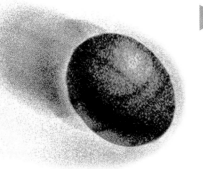

▶ Making Connections

MAKE A LIST

Allie decides she wants to be a professional basketball player. In "To . . . ," the poet wants to become a writer. Think of a job you might like to have when you get older. Make a list of the reasons you would want this job.

▶ Play It Safe

CREATE A POSTER

Playing sports and outdoor games is fun, but it is important to play safely. Did you notice the picture of Allie's friend on a skateboard? He is wearing safety gear to protect him in case he falls. Think of another activity that needs safety gear. Create a poster that shows the gear and explains why it is needed.

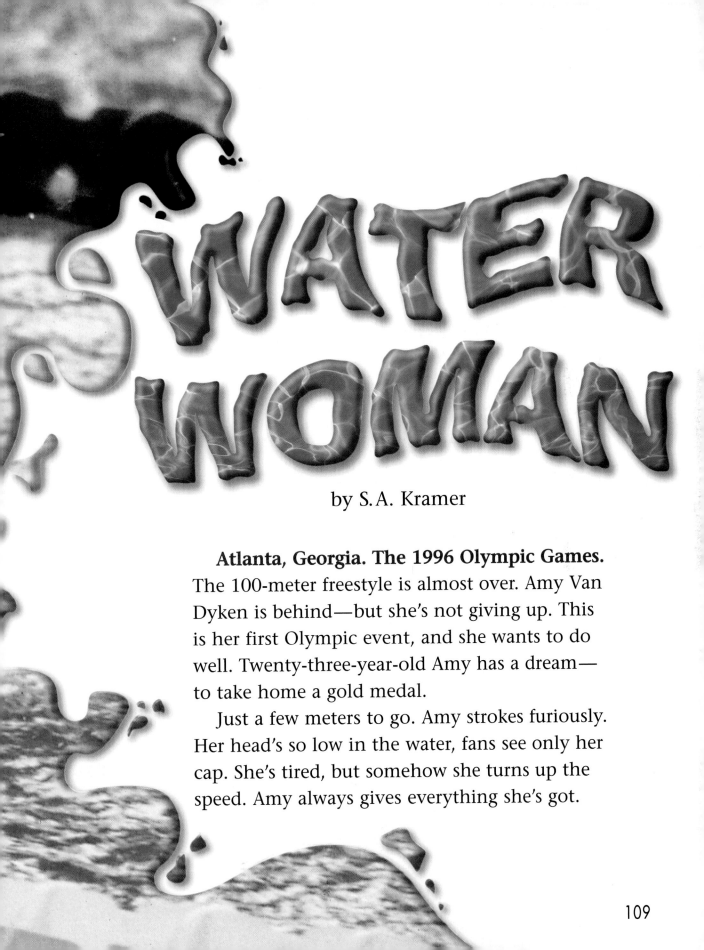

WATER WOMAN

by S. A. Kramer

Atlanta, Georgia. The 1996 Olympic Games.
The 100-meter freestyle is almost over. Amy Van Dyken is behind—but she's not giving up. This is her first Olympic event, and she wants to do well. Twenty-three-year-old Amy has a dream—to take home a gold medal.

Just a few meters to go. Amy strokes furiously. Her head's so low in the water, fans see only her cap. She's tired, but somehow she turns up the speed. Amy always gives everything she's got.

This time it's not enough. Amy finishes fourth. No gold, no silver—not even a bronze. But as she leaves the pool, she isn't thinking about losing. Her burst of speed has made her muscles cramp. The pain is so bad, she can't even stand.

Amy falls to the pool deck. Cramps shoot into her back and neck. She gasps for air. Trainers have to carry her off on a stretcher.

What a way to start the Olympics! Amy can't believe her bad luck. But it's not the first time her health has gotten in her way.

Ever since she was little, Amy's had asthma (you say it like this: AZ-mah). Asthma is an illness that makes it hard to breathe. Amy's lungs have never worked right.

As a child, she was always out of breath. Climbing just one flight of stairs left her huffing and puffing. But when she was seven, her doctor said swimming might help her. So Amy headed straight for the pool.

Her talent didn't show right away—far from it. Even at twelve, she could hardly finish a race. She'd often have to stop in the middle to catch her breath.

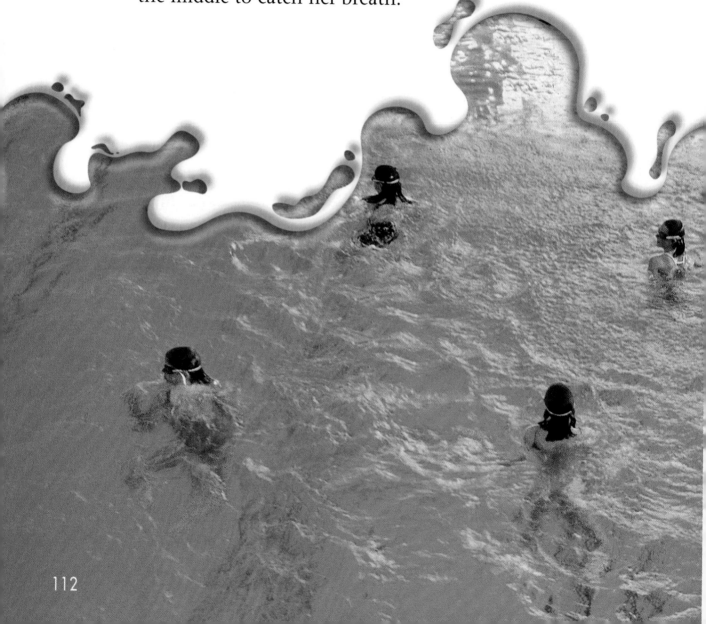

Things weren't much better in high school. Amy coughed all the time. She was also awkward, skinny—and six feet tall! Her classmates made fun of her. Amy felt like a nerd.

Somehow she made the school swim team. But then the coach put her on a relay with three other girls.

The girls weren't happy. They complained to the coach. To get Amy to quit, they threw her clothes into the pool. . . .

Amy felt awful. But she didn't leave the team. Later she said, "I'm really stubborn. If someone tells me I stink, I'm going to try to prove them wrong." She vowed that one day she'd make those girls respect her.

In college at Colorado State, Amy joined the swim team. Fighting her asthma, she got all the way to the 1990 junior nationals. But she wasn't fast enough to make the 1992 Olympic team.

Amy kept trying. She got faster and faster. But in 1993, she flopped in the NCAA championships. And after that, she caught a terrible virus.

Amy was depressed. All her training hadn't made her a champion. She told herself, "This is too hard. I want to be normal." For a few months she quit swimming. But she didn't stay away for long. She missed it too much.

Amy charged back into the pool. She learned to make her starts faster and to stroke with more power. To boost her speed, she kept shaving the hair off her body. She said, "If I miss the hair on my knee, it could cost me a hundredth of a second."

Her all-out attitude paid off. In the 1994 world championships, she won a bronze medal in the 50-meter freestyle. The same year, she was named female NCAA swimmer of the year. Then in 1995, she broke the U.S. records for both the 50-meter and 50-yard freestyle.

Amy was on a roll. In 1996 she won a place on the Olympic team. This time none of her teammates complained. In fact, she became their leader. Her horrible high school years seemed long ago.

Now she's at the Olympic games, lying on a stretcher. Her teammates are worried. But Amy has come back from worse. She calls herself "the tough girl." Sure enough, two hours later her cramps ease up and she's feeling fine.

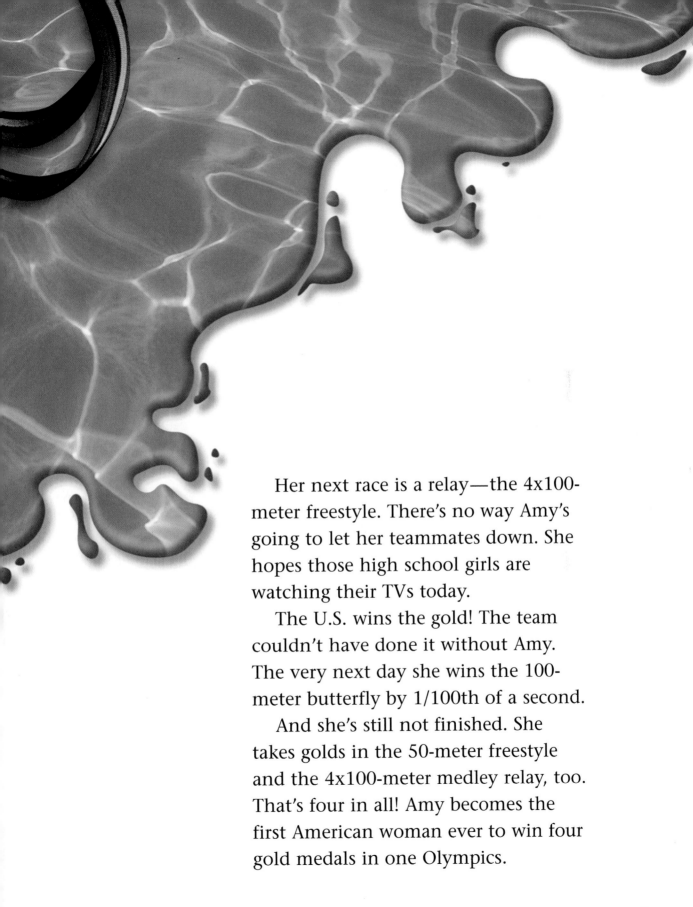

Her next race is a relay—the 4x100-meter freestyle. There's no way Amy's going to let her teammates down. She hopes those high school girls are watching their TVs today.

The U.S. wins the gold! The team couldn't have done it without Amy. The very next day she wins the 100-meter butterfly by 1/100th of a second.

And she's still not finished. She takes golds in the 50-meter freestyle and the 4x100-meter medley relay, too. That's four in all! Amy becomes the first American woman ever to win four gold medals in one Olympics.

No one makes fun of Amy anymore. In fact, she's almost too popular. Fans won't leave her alone. At hotels, she uses a fake name so strangers can't keep calling her.

Her asthma still makes her sick. Some days, she has to stay out of the water. When she pushes herself too hard, she ends up in the hospital. Even now, Amy takes medicine three times a day.

She often thinks about her future. She may teach biology or work with deaf children. But one thing she knows for sure. Swimming will always be part of her life.

THINK ABOUT IT

1 What things made it difficult for Amy Van Dyken to become a champion swimmer?

2 Would you want to have Amy Van Dyken for a friend? Explain your answer.

3 Why do you think the author told about Amy's childhood as well as her time at the Olympics?

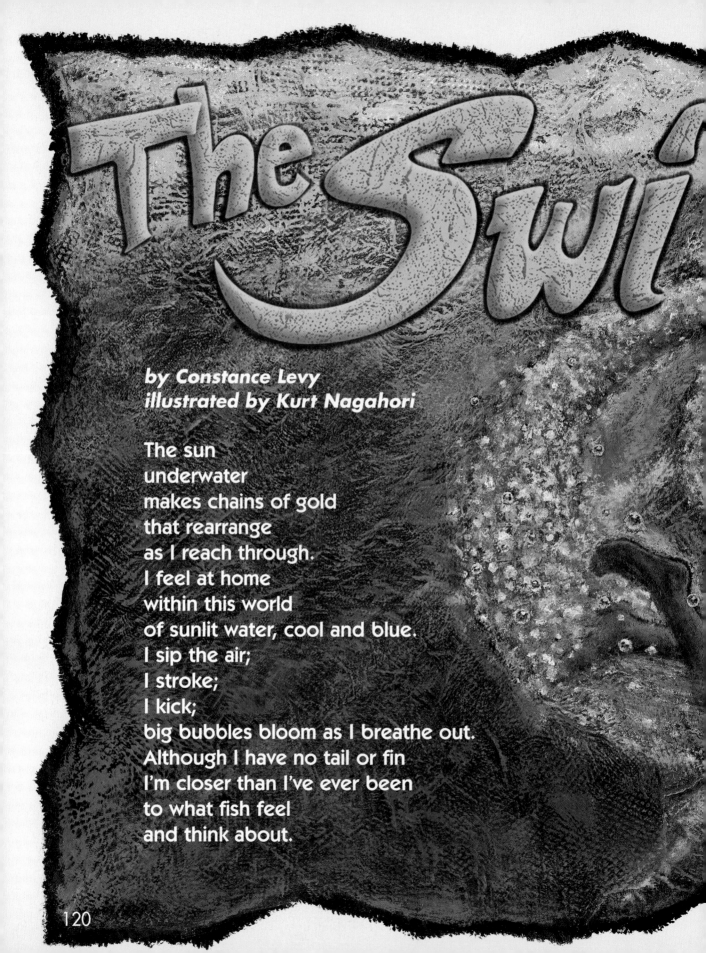

The Swi

by Constance Levy
illustrated by Kurt Nagahori

The sun
underwater
makes chains of gold
that rearrange
as I reach through.
I feel at home
within this world
of sunlit water, cool and blue.
I sip the air;
I stroke;
I kick;
big bubbles bloom as I breathe out.
Although I have no tail or fin
I'm closer than I've ever been
to what fish feel
and think about.

mmer

Response

What a Worker!

WRITE A LIST

Amy Van Dyken works hard. We know this because the story tells us she "always gives everything she's got." Make a list of examples from the story that prove she is a hard worker.

My Hero

PRESENT A REPORT

For swimmers everywhere, Amy Van Dyken is a hero. She won more gold medals in Atlanta than any American woman ever had. Who is your hero? Find out about someone you think is a hero, and present a report to your classmates.

Activities

Come One, Come All

MAKE A POSTER

Imagine that your school is having a Field Day. There will be races, jumping competitions, and other kinds of fun! How can you use pictures to tell people about it? Create a poster that will make people want to come to the Field Day.

Making Connections

DESCRIBE AN EVENT

In "The Swimmer," you read the words *sunlit water, cool and blue*. The poet wants us to feel the cool water and see the sun shining through it. In "Water Woman," you read *Amy strokes furiously*. We can imagine her arms moving very quickly. Write a description of a sports event so that the reader can imagine what is happening.

THEME WRAP-UP

Such Characters!

MAKE A CHART Think about the main characters in the stories, poems, and article. How would you describe each character? Would you use words like *friendly*, *shy*, *talented*, or *smart*? Make a chart that tells about each character. Your chart may look like the one here. Check the boxes that tell what each character is like.

	Friendly	Shy	Talented	Smart
Arthur				
Marta				
Ronald				
Allie				
Amy				

Your Favorites

DISCUSS QUESTIONS

With a small group, discuss the selections in this theme. Talk about questions like these:

- Which is your favorite selection? Why?

- Which characters are the most interesting?

- Are there any words or sentences you want to remember?

- How are the stories, poems, and article alike? How are they different?

What Is the Message?

AUTHOR'S MESSAGES

The title of this theme is "Something Special!" Choose two selections from the theme. Write a few sentences about what you think each author is telling you about being special.

What a Team!

126

Contents

Reader's

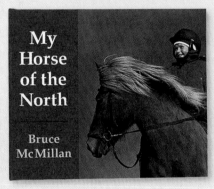

My Horse of the North
by Bruce McMillan

NONFICTION

A girl and her horse learn how to work together in Iceland.

Award-Winning Author and Photographer

READER'S CHOICE LIBRARY

Ibis, a True Whale Story
by John Himmelman

INFORMATIONAL STORY

A young humpback whale is hurt. Can her human friends help her?

Award-Winning Author
READER'S CHOICE LIBRARY

Choice

Seal Surfer
by *Michael Foreman*

FICTION

A boy and a seal
watch out for each other
as the seasons pass.

***SLJ* Best Book**

The Goat in the Rug
by *Charles L. Blood and Martin Link*

INFORMATIONAL STORY

A wooly goat helps her
friend weave a beautiful rug.

Nell Nugget and the Cow Caper
by *Judith Ross Enderle and
Stephanie Gordon Tessler*

TALL TALE

Nell's best cow is missing! Brave Nell sets
out on a wild adventure to find Goldie.

129

OFFICER BUCKLE
AND
GLORIA

BY
PEGGY RATHMANN

Caldecott
Medal

NEVER FLY KITES NEAR POWER LINES.

NEVER PLAY LOUD MUSIC INTO HEADPHONES.

NEVER EAT RAW HAMBURGER.

NEVER TILT YOUR CHAIR BACK ON TWO LEGS.

Officer Buckle knew more safety tips than anyone else in Napville. Every time he thought of a new one, he thumbtacked it to his bulletin board.

Safety Tip #77

NEVER stand on a SWIVEL CHAIR.

133

Officer Buckle shared his safety tips
with the students at Napville School.
Nobody ever listened. Sometimes,
there was snoring.

Afterward, it was business as usual. Mrs. Toppel, the principal, took down the welcome banner. "NEVER stand on a SWIVEL CHAIR," said Officer Buckle, but Mrs. Toppel didn't hear him.

Then one day, Napville's police department bought a police dog named Gloria. When it was time for Officer Buckle to give the safety speech at the school, Gloria went along.

"Children, this is Gloria," announced Officer Buckle. "Gloria obeys my commands. Gloria, SIT!" And Gloria sat.

Officer Buckle gave Safety Tip Number One: "KEEP your SHOELACES tied!" The children sat up and stared.

Officer Buckle checked to see if Gloria was sitting at attention. She was.

"Safety Tip Number Two," said Officer Buckle.
"ALWAYS wipe up spills BEFORE someone
SLIPS AND FALLS!"
The children's eyes popped.
Officer Buckle checked on Gloria again.
"Good dog," he said.

Officer Buckle thought of a safety tip he had discovered that morning.

"NEVER leave a THUMBTACK where you might SIT on it!"

The audience roared.

Officer Buckle grinned. He said the rest of the tips with *plenty* of expression.

The children clapped their hands and cheered. Some of them laughed until they cried.

Officer Buckle was surprised. He had never noticed how funny safety tips could be. After this safety speech, there wasn't a single accident.

The next day, an enormous envelope arrived at the police station. It was stuffed with thank-you letters from the students at Napville School.

Every letter had a drawing of Gloria on it. Officer Buckle thought the drawings showed a lot of imagination. His favorite letter was written on a star-shaped piece of paper. It said:

Dear Gloria and Officer Buckle,
Thanks for coming to our school.
You are nice.
Your friend,
George

Dear Gloria and Officer Buckle,
Here is a picture of
Come back soon! Your friend

Dear Gloria and Officer Buckle,
you for ias the ria, Tips. aunt back soon. dog and med him er me. I like dogs and safety
Your friend, Andrew

You and Gloria make a good team.
Your friend,
Claire

P.S. I always wear a crash helmet.
(Safety Tip #7)

#1 KEEP SHOE- LACES TIED

DISPOSE OF WAMA PROPERLY

Officer Buckle was thumbtacking Claire's letter to his bulletin board when the phones started ringing. Grade schools, high schools, and day-care centers were calling about the safety speech.

"Officer Buckle," they said, "our students want to hear your safety tips! And please, bring along that police dog."

Officer Buckle told his safety tips to 313 schools. Everywhere he and Gloria went, children sat up and listened.

After every speech, Officer Buckle took Gloria out for ice cream. Officer Buckle loved having a buddy.

Then one day, a television news team videotaped Officer Buckle in the state-college auditorium. When he finished Safety Tip Number Ninety-nine, DO NOT GO SWIMMING DURING ELECTRICAL STORMS!, the students jumped to their feet and applauded.

"Bravo! Bravo!" they cheered.
Officer Buckle bowed again and again.

That night, Officer Buckle watched himself on the 10 o'clock news.

The next day, the principal of Napville School telephoned the police station. "Good morning, Officer Buckle! It's time for our safety speech!"

Officer Buckle frowned.

"I'm not giving any more speeches! Nobody looks at me, anyway!"

"Oh," said Mrs. Toppel. "Well! How about Gloria? Could she come?"

Someone else from the police station gave Gloria a ride to the school. Gloria sat onstage looking lonely. Then she fell asleep. So did the audience.

145

After Gloria left, Napville School had its
biggest accident ever. . . .

It started with a puddle of banana pudding. . . .
SPLAT! SPLATTER!
SPLOOSH! Everyone slid smack into
Mrs. Toppel,
who screamed
and let go of her hammer.

147

The next morning, a pile of letters arrived at the police station.

Every letter had a drawing of the accident.

Officer Buckle was shocked.

At the bottom of the pile was a note written on a paper star.

Officer Buckle smiled.

The note said:

Gloria missed you yesterday!
Your friend,
Claire

P.S. Don't worry, I was wearing my helmet! (Safety Tip #7)

Gloria gave Officer Buckle a big kiss on the nose. Officer Buckle gave Gloria a nice pat on the back. Then, Officer Buckle thought of his best safety tip yet . . .

Safety Tip #101

"ALWAYS STICK WITH YOUR BUDDY!"

Think About It

1 What makes Gloria and Officer Buckle a good team?

2 What is your favorite part of this story? Explain why.

3 How is Gloria like a real dog? How is she different?

Meet the Author and Illustrator
PEGGY RATHMANN

Peggy Rathmann was not always sure that she wanted to be a writer and an artist. In college, she wanted to teach sign language to gorillas. She changed her mind and thought about being a doctor. In fact, she changed her mind a lot.

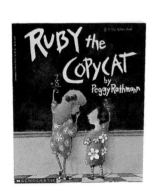

CHECK HOW DEEP THE WATER IS BEFORE YOU DIVE.

Finally, she realized that she had a talent for art. Her family and friends had known *that* for a long time! She took a class that taught her how to put her art and her story-writing together. Finding good ideas for stories was not easy. Peggy Rathmann's teacher told her to try writing about things that were important to her. That advice worked so well that she still follows it every time she writes! Where do you think the ideas for *Officer Buckle and Gloria* came from?

NEVER GIVE INFORMATION OVER THE PHONE TO STRANGERS.

Peggy Rathmann wrote about a girl like herself in her first book, *Ruby the Copycat*.

Visit *The Learning Site!*
www.harcourtschool.com

Safety is very important to Peggy Rathmann. She likes to share safety information with her family and friends. It is not surprising that Officer Buckle is also very careful.

Peggy Rathmann loves dogs and other animals. Her family once had a pet dog named Skippy. He was a good dog, but sometimes he got into trouble when he thought no one was looking. The family found out about Skippy's secrets when they saw their dog on a videotape. Skippy was helping himself to breakfast from the kitchen table! Do you think that Gloria and Skippy are alike?

"Aunt Peggy is a very careful person. Not only is she careful for herself, she is careful for everyone else."

—*Robin Rathmann*
(Ms. Rathmann's niece)

RESPONSE ACTIVITIES

 A SAFETY SPEECH

GIVE A SPEECH

Work with a partner to create a safety speech that is fun to watch. Choose five safety tips from the story to tell about. Think of ways to make the speech fun for listeners. For example, you and your partner could sing a song or do a dance as part of your speech.

DOG HEROES ★

WRITE A REPORT

Gloria helps Officer Buckle teach people about safety. Learn about some other ways that dogs help people. You might find out about police dogs, rescue dogs, or guide dogs. Look in books about dogs. Write a short report about what you learn.

STAYING SAFE

MAKE A POSTER

Make a safety poster for your classroom or school. Use some of the safety tips from the story, and add some of your own. Draw a picture for each tip. Ask if you can display the poster somewhere in your school.

BUDDIES FOREVER

WRITE A POEM

Officer Buckle thinks the best safety tip ever is "Always stick with your buddy!" Write a poem about buddies. Before you start, think about these questions: What can buddies do together? How can buddies help each other?

Story Elements

Like all stories, "Officer Buckle and Gloria" has three important parts, or elements. The **setting** is when and where the story takes place. The **characters** are the people and animals you meet in the story. The **plot** is what happens in the story. This story map shows the three main parts of the story "Officer Buckle and Gloria."

Setting

now, the present time
in Napville

Characters

Officer Buckle, Gloria,
Mrs. Toppel, Claire

Plot

Problem

Students pay more attention to Gloria than to Officer Buckle.

Important Events

- Gloria acts out Officer Buckle's safety tips when he isn't looking.
- Officer Buckle is sad when he finds out what Gloria is doing. He decides not to give any more speeches.
- Gloria tries to give a speech without Officer Buckle.

Solution

Officer Buckle realizes that both he and Gloria are important. The two of them work together again as a team.

Looking for the problems that the characters face, and the solutions, will help you understand the plot of the story. Knowing a story's setting can help you imagine when and where the story takes place. Noticing what a character says and does can help you better understand the character's actions.

Read this story beginning. What is the setting? Who are the characters? Tell what you think the problem in this story might be.

Reggie walked slowly into the barn. There, lying beside the cow, was a huge dog. The dog stood up and faced Reggie.

"Is that your pet dog?" Reggie asked his cousin Joel. Reggie had never seen such a large dog. "I know a lot about computer games, but I have no idea how to get along with a dog that's as big as a horse!" he said.

WHAT HAVE YOU LEARNED?

1. Think about a story you have read. How would the story be different if it had a different setting?

2. Imagine you are writing a story. Decide the setting, characters, and plot for your story.

TRY THIS   TRY THIS   TRY THIS

Choose a story you enjoy or one that you have read recently. Make a story map like the one on page 154 to tell the setting and to describe the characters and the plot of the story.

Visit *The Learning Site!*
www.harcourtschool.com

Turtle Bay

by **SAVIOUR PIROTTA**
pictures by **NILESH MISTRY**

Notable
Trade Book in
Social Studies

Outstanding
Science
Trade Book

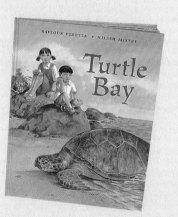

SAVIOUR PIROTTA • NILESH MISTRY

Turtle
Bay

Taro and Jiro-San were friends.

Jiro-San showed Taro how to feed crabs with pieces of rotten fish. He taught him to dive for sponges. When the sea was too rough for swimming, he trained him to sit very still and watch the sea horses swim around the seaweed in the deeper rock pools.

Taro's sister, Yuko, didn't like Jiro-San.

"He's weird," she said. "Last year my friends saw him sweeping the beach with a broom."

"No, he's not," said Taro. "He's old and wise, and full of wonderful secrets."

One day, Taro found Jiro-San sitting on a big rock. "What are you doing?" he asked.

"I am listening," said Jiro-San. "The wind is bringing me a message." Taro sat on the rock and listened. But all he could hear was the seagulls crying.

"Ah," said Jiro-San at last. "Now I understand . . . My old friends are coming."

"Who are your old friends?" asked Taro.

"You'll see," said Jiro-San.

Next day, Jiro-San brought two brooms and handed one to Taro.

"For sweeping the beach," he said.

Taro's heart sank. Yuko was right after all—Jiro-San was weird.

"There's a lot of rubbish and broken glass on the beach," Jiro-San explained. "My friends won't come if there is broken glass. They know they'll get hurt."

The boy and the old man swept the beach from one end to the other. They collected all the rubbish and put it in Jiro-San's cart. Soon the beach was cleaner than it had been all summer.

Jiro-San looked pleased.

"Meet me by the big rock tonight," he told Taro.

Taro ate his supper as fast as he could.

"You seem in a big hurry," said his mother.

"I am," said Taro. "Jiro-San's old friends are coming."

"Who are they?" his mother wanted to know.

"It's a secret," said Taro.

"What kind of secret?" Yuko asked.

Taro didn't answer. He washed his hands and went out to find Jiro-San.

"Look," said the old man, pointing out to sea. Taro saw a school of dolphins riding the waves.

"Are they your old friends?" he asked.

"No," said Jiro-San. "Perhaps they will come tomorrow night."

Taro waited patiently all the next day. In the evening, he met Jiro-San again. This time, the old man had brought his boat out of the shed. Jiro-San picked up the oars, and they pushed out to sea.

After a while, the old man said, "We've got company." Taro watched as a huge whale flicked her tail up out of the water. She had a calf swimming beside her.

"Are they your old friends?" Taro asked.

"They're friends," said Jiro-San, "but not the old friends I meant. Maybe they will come tomorrow."

The next evening, Jiro-San was in his boat again.

"Where are we going?" Taro wanted to know.

"Over there," said Jiro-San. He rowed out to a secret cove on a little island. There Taro saw three large fish with swords for snouts.

"Are they your old friends?" Taro asked.

"All fish are my friends," said Jiro-San. "But these aren't my old friends. They seem to be late this year. Perhaps they are not coming at all."

"Don't be sad," Taro said. "Perhaps they'll get here tomorrow."

"Do you want to come and wait for Jiro-San's old friends?" Taro asked Yuko after supper the next day. Yuko wasn't doing anything, so she followed Taro to the big rocks, kicking the sand as she walked.

"Ssshh," said Jiro-San. "I think they're here at last." Yuko and Taro saw a dark shape moving toward the shore. It was huge and bobbed up and down on the water like an enormous cork.

At last, the children could see what it was—a turtle!

"She's coming to lay her eggs on our beach," said Jiro-San proudly.

The turtle scrambled ashore and started digging with her flippers. When the hole was deep enough, she laid almost a hundred round, creamy-colored eggs in the nest. Then she filled in the hole with her hind flippers, flung more sand over it with her front flippers, and hurried back to the sea.

"She is going to tell the others," said Jiro-San.

"What is she going to tell them?" asked Yuko.

"That the beach is safe," said Taro happily.

The next day, Yuko came to the beach with her own broom.

"Can I help sweep the sand?" she asked.

"Of course," said Jiro-San. "The more of us there are, the safer the beach will be for the turtles."

The three friends swept up all the litter dropped by the beachgoers during the day. Then they sat on the rocks and watched more turtles coming ashore. There were lots of them, all huge and old and wise—just like Jiro-San.

"Now," said Jiro-San, "you must be patient, and wait until you hear from me again."

Eight weeks later, Jiro-San told the children to meet him at dusk.

"Sit on the rocks, please," he said, "and watch the ground."

The children looked and waited for what seemed like hours. As the moon rose, they saw something moving under the sand—something small and fast and eager.

"It's a baby turtle!" cried Taro. "The eggs have hatched!"

Soon the beach was full of baby turtles. There were hundreds of them, all scuttling down to the sea.

The children couldn't believe their eyes.

"Jiro-San is not crazy after all, is he?" Taro whispered to Yuko.

"No," said Yuko. "He is old and wise . . . and full of wonderful secrets."

THINK ABOUT IT

1. How do Jiro-San, Taro, and Yuko help the turtles? Why do they do this?

2. Would you have helped Jiro-San clean the beach? Tell why or why not.

3. What kind of person is Jiro-San? How can you tell?

Meet the Author
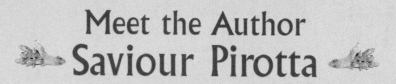
Saviour Pirotta

Saviour Pirotta's life as a writer began when he started writing plays for children. He read these plays on the radio in Malta, the island country in the Mediterranean Sea where he was born. Later, he moved to London, England.

Before he became a children's author, Saviour Pirotta worked as a storyteller. He told stories at many schools and libraries around England and became very well known. He has even told a story to Queen Elizabeth.

Now Saviour Pirotta has written many children's books. He says he likes to write books that teach children about things. When he has time, he visits schools to help children make their own picture books.

Visit *The Learning Site!* www.harcourtschool.com

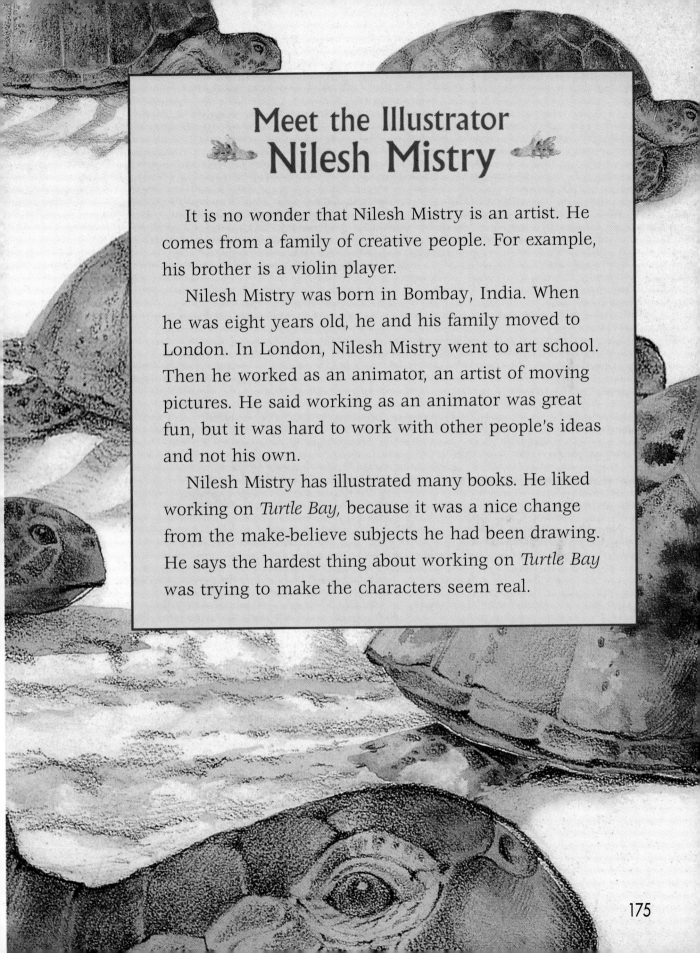

Meet the Illustrator
Nilesh Mistry

It is no wonder that Nilesh Mistry is an artist. He comes from a family of creative people. For example, his brother is a violin player.

Nilesh Mistry was born in Bombay, India. When he was eight years old, he and his family moved to London. In London, Nilesh Mistry went to art school. Then he worked as an animator, an artist of moving pictures. He said working as an animator was great fun, but it was hard to work with other people's ideas and not his own.

Nilesh Mistry has illustrated many books. He liked working on *Turtle Bay,* because it was a nice change from the make-believe subjects he had been drawing. He says the hardest thing about working on *Turtle Bay* was trying to make the characters seem real.

DREAM BOAT

by Charles Ghigna
illustrated by Dave Calver

If I could build a sailing ship,
And I could have one wish,
I'd want my helpers all to be
Dolphins, whales, and fish.

The Sawfish would saw all the boards
And cut the mast and rails;
The shark known as the Hammerhead,
Of course, would drive the nails.

For lights I'd use, if it agrees,
The bright Electric Eel;
The Dolphin with its dorsal fin
Would be the sailboat's keel.

I'd ask the Sailfish if it minds
Serving as the sail;
And for the anchor I would need
The giant Humpback Whale!

The captain of the sailing ship
(If I could have my wish)
Would be the one who sails the best—
The clever Pilotfish.

Response Activities

How I Spent My Summer Vacation

WRITE A REPORT

Imagine that you are Taro or Yuko. What would you tell your classmates about how you spent the last school break? Write a short report telling about some of the things you did. You might also write about some of the amazing animals you saw.

Let's Clean Up!

WRITE A PLAN

Jiro-San, Taro, and Yuko clean the beach for the turtles. With a partner, think of a place that you could clean up, such as a beach, a park, or your schoolyard. Make a cleanup plan. Don't forget to tell how many people and what supplies you would need.

Making Connections

ADD TO A POEM

"Dream Boat" tells how different sea creatures help build and sail a ship. Write two more verses for the poem. Tell how some of the creatures in "Turtle Bay," such as the swordfish and sea turtles, could help.

Sea Life

MAKE A COLLAGE

Taro admires all the ocean creatures he sees. Make a collage showing different kinds of sea animals. Draw the pictures, or cut photos of sea creatures from old magazines. Paste the pictures on a sheet of paper. Write the name of each animal below its picture.

WILD

SHOTS,
They're My Life

from *Ranger Rick Magazine*

"Hey, you don't scare me," this Galapagos penguin seems to be saying. But who *is* that strange, masked creature?

by Tui De Roy

When I was a little girl, all my best friends were furry, feathered, or scaly! My friends were the gentle, trusting creatures of the Galapagos (gə·lä´pə·gəs) Islands, where I grew up.

In those days there was no school nearby, so my mom taught my little brother and me at home. But my favorite classroom was the great Galapagos outdoors! The islands were formed long ago by a bunch of volcanoes far out in the Pacific Ocean. My family moved to the islands from Europe when I was only two.

The creature behind the face mask (on page 181) is me. Most of the time, you'll find me behind a camera. Come see the world through my eyes.

When I was 10, my dad let me use his old camera. Right away, I started snapping photos of my animal friends. And in the 30 years since then, I've never stopped.

The best part was that the animals in the Galapagos were as curious about me as I was about them. That's why I was able to get "up close and personal" with the Galapagos hawks shown here. See the shot I got? **(above)**

Like I said, I'm still taking lots of wildlife photos, and my best friends are still furry, feathered, and scaly. But now I find them all over the world, not just in the Galapagos.

I like to photograph animals best when they're minding their own business—not watching me. That means I have to spend a lot of time with them until they get so used to me that they forget I'm there.

Now let me tell you about some of my favorite photos— and the adventures I had getting them.

ENOUGH, ALREADY!

The king penguin chick **below** looks like it's wearing a furry overcoat. But that's just its thick, downy baby feathers. They work like a coat to keep the chick warm.

The chick was bugging its parents, begging for food. They finally got tired of being pestered and started waddling away. But the chick kept right up with them, and I had to scurry to get this shot.

HEY, OUTTA MY WAY!

The Galapagos Islands are famous for their huge tortoises. In fact, *galapagos* means "tortoises" in Spanish. When early Spanish-speaking explorers came to the islands, they saw *tons* of these big fellas.

One day I was nose to nose with one, with just a camera between us **(top)**. The tortoise was so busy looking for just the right tasty plants, it acted as if I weren't even there. I had to move out of *its* way before it bumped right into me! But look at the kind of action shot you can snap by getting down with your subject **(above)**. *CHOMP.* Tortoises love a good cactus. Never mind the spines!

INTO THE WASH

Galapagos marine iguanas (i·gwä′nəz) are the only lizards in the world that feed in the sea. Usually they graze on stubby seaweed that grows along the wave-beaten shoreline.

I wanted to show how these little sea dragons are right at home in the pounding waves. But to do it, I had to get in there with them! First I put my camera into a waterproof case with a clear front clamped on. Then I crept toward my target **(above)**. Iguanas have sharp claws, so they can hang on tight to rocks in the surf. What about me? I bounced around and got lots of cuts and bruises. But this neat photo **(right)** was worth it!

DUELING DUOS

Watching animals fight can be pretty wild—and scary. But usually it looks worse than it is: The fighters almost never hurt each other seriously.

Look at the two male frigate birds in the big photo **above**. They were squabbling Galapagos neighbors, snapping at each other with their sharp beaks. But neither delicate throat pouch got punctured. (The male on the right had his pouch puffed out, showing off to the females flying overhead.)

The fight in the **lower** photo was between elephant seal bulls on an island near Antarctica. I saw these guys having it out from way down the beach. They were so wrapped up in who would be beach-master, they didn't notice me getting close. (But not *too* close. Each bull was taller than me and outweighed me by a couple of tons!)

In a few months, her babies would hatch and, with luck, head out to sea too. The ones that survived would spend years growing up far out in the ocean. Then someday the females would return to this beach to lay their eggs.

Like the sea turtles, I return to the shores of the Galapagos Islands from time to time too. There are always new animal friends to meet there.

All of a sudden, they reared up and flashed their "fangs." *CLICK*—got it! I had to be really quick. The next second, they were back to their lazy pushing and shoving. Finally, they collapsed into a heap and started snoozing.

HOMECOMING

The shot **above** was taken at sunrise on a Galapagos beach. The green turtle was crawling back down to the sea. She had spent the night burying her eggs in the sand.

Think About It

1 How do animals help the author make a living?

2 How would you feel about getting very close to wild animals, as the author does?

3 How can you tell that the author likes animals?

RESPONSE ACTIVITIES

TURTLE TALK

ROLE-PLAY AN INTERVIEW

Suppose a reporter interviewed Tui De Roy. What questions would he or she ask? With a partner, role-play an interview. You can write the questions and answers together. Then one of you can ask the questions, and the other can answer. Use information from the story to help you.

FUR, FEATHERS, SCALES

MAKE A CHART

When she was little, the photographer's best friends were "furry, feathered, or scaly." Make a chart that has three headings—**Furry, Feathered,** and **Scaly.** List at least three different animals that belong in each group. Start with animals from this selection. Also look for animals in a science book or in magazines about nature.

WHERE ON EARTH?

DRAW A MAP

The author grew up on the Galapagos Islands. Use an encyclopedia or the Internet to get information about the Galapagos Islands. Draw a map showing where they are. Below the map, write facts about the Galapagos Islands.

WORKING WITH ANIMALS

MAKE A LIST

Tui De Roy earns a living taking photographs of animals. Make a list of other jobs that have to do with animals, such as zookeeper, vet, and animal trainer. If you could have one of these jobs, which one would you choose? Why? Circle the job and write your reasons next to it.

Vocabulary in Context

In "Wild Shots, They're My Life," you read about *marine iguanas*. You used what you know about letters and sounds to read those words. However, maybe you had never heard of marine iguanas. You might have looked for clues to help you understand what they are. The sentences below, from the article, have clues you might have used.

clue

Galapagos marine iguanas are the only lizards in the world that feed in the sea. I wanted to show how these little sea dragons are right at home in the pounding waves.

clue

When you look at the words and sentences that are near a new word, you are using **context clues.** After you have sounded out a word, finding context clues can help you understand its meaning.

You can use context clues to learn the meanings of science words or words in other subjects. Read the paragraph below. What context clues help you figure out what a *carapace* is?

Every turtle has a shell made of two parts, top and bottom. When you look at a turtle's back, you will see that its carapace is covered with markings of spots, swirls, or colors. This hard, leathery top section helps protect a turtle's soft body.

WHAT HAVE YOU LEARNED?

1. One part of the article, "Wild Shots, They're My Life," is called "Homecoming." What does *homecoming* mean? What clues helped you understand the word?

2. Imagine you are reading a book about sea life. You come across the word *pinniped*. What can you do to help you understand what a pinniped is?

TRY THIS • TRY THIS • TRY THIS

Look in your science or social studies textbook to find a new, unfamiliar word. Use what you know about letters and sounds to say the word. Use context clues to figure out the meaning of the word. Write the word and what you think it means. Then use the book's glossary or a dictionary to check the meaning.

Visit *The Learning Site!*
www.harcourtschool.com

BALTO, THE DOG
WHO SAVED NOME

by Margaret Davidson ● illustrations by Doug Rugh

"THIS IS NOME, ALASKA. REPEAT. THIS IS NOME, ALASKA. WE NEED HELP. FAST . . ."

A man bent over the machine in the Nome telegraph office. Again and again he pressed down the signal key. *Click-click-clack . . . Clack-click-clack . . .* He was sending a message to the town of Anchorage, Alaska, 800 miles to the southeast.

Click-click-clack . . . Clack-click-clack . . . The Anchorage telegraph operator wrote down the message. The news was very bad.

A terrible sickness had broken out in the Nome area—a disease called diphtheria. Some people had already died of it. Many more would die if they weren't treated soon.

There was no medicine to treat diphtheria in Nome. The medicine they needed would have to come from Anchorage—800 miles away—through a wild wind and snow storm. The storm was so bad that airplanes couldn't fly through it. Trains couldn't get through either. Nome was very near the sea, but the sea was frozen solid. And the road from the south was completely blocked by deep drifts of snow.

There was only one way to get the medicine from Anchorage to Nome—by dogsled.

ALASKA

The medicine was packed in a box and sent north by
train—as far as a train could go on the snowy tracks. It was
still more than 600 miles south of Nome. From now on teams
of dogs would have to take it the rest of the way.

The teams were ready. The first team pushed north
through the storm to a little town. There a second team was
waiting. It went on to another small town where a third team
was ready to take the medicine farther.

At first the teams managed to go many miles before they grew tired. But the storm was growing worse by the minute. Finally Charlie Olson's team staggered into the little village of Bluff—60 miles from Nome. They had only gone 20 miles, yet Olson and the dogs were almost frozen and completely worn out.

Gunnar Kasson and his team were waiting in Bluff. The wind screamed through the little town. The snow was piling up deeper and deeper on the ground. It was 30 degrees *below* zero Fahrenheit outside now. And the temperature was falling fast.

"It's no use trying to go out in *that*," Charlie Olson said. "I almost didn't make it. You and the dogs will freeze solid before you get half way."

But Kasson knew how important the medicine was. He knew that hundreds—maybe thousands—of people would die if they didn't get the medicine soon. Besides, he knew he didn't have to go all the way. Another team was waiting 40 miles away in the little village of Safety. That team would take the medicine the last 20 miles to Nome.

Quickly Gunnar Kasson hitched up his team of dogs. And at the head of the long line he put his lead dog, Balto.

Balto was a mixed-breed. He was half Eskimo dog—and half wolf. Many dogs who are part wolf never become tame. They never learn to trust people—or obey them either. Balto was different. He was a gentle dog who obeyed orders quickly. He also knew how to think for himself.

Usually Gunnar Kasson guided the dogs. He told them where to go. Now he couldn't even see his hand in front of his face. So everything was up to Balto. The big black dog would have to find the trail by smell. Then he'd have to stay on it no matter what happened.

Gunnar Kasson climbed onto the back of the sled. He cracked his whip in the air. *"Mush!"* he cried. *"Move out!"*

The first part of the trail to Nome led across the sea ice.
This ice wasn't anything like ice on a small pond or lake.
It seemed much more *alive*. And no wonder. The water *under*
the ice was moving up and down because of the storm. So
the ice was moving up and down too. Up and down, up and
down it went, like a roller coaster.

In some places the ice was smooth—as smooth and slippery as glass. Dogs are usually sure-footed. But they slipped and skidded across this ice. So did the sled.

And sometimes the ice came to sharp points—points that dug deep into the dogs' paws.

Worst of all were the places where the ice was bumpy—so bumpy that the sled turned over again and again. Each time it turned over, the other dogs began to bark and snap at each other. But Balto always stood quietly while Kasson set the sled upright again. Balto was calm, so the other dogs grew calmer too.

The team had been moving across the ice for hours. Suddenly there was a loud *cracking* sound—like a gun going off. Kasson knew that sound. It was the sound of ice breaking. Somewhere not far ahead the ice had split apart. If the team kept going straight they would run right into the freezing water—and drown.

Balto heard the ice crack too. He slowed for a moment. Then he turned left. He headed straight out to sea. He went for a long time. Then he turned right once more.

Balto was leading the team *around* the icy water. Finally he gave a sharp bark and turned north. He had found the trail to Nome again.

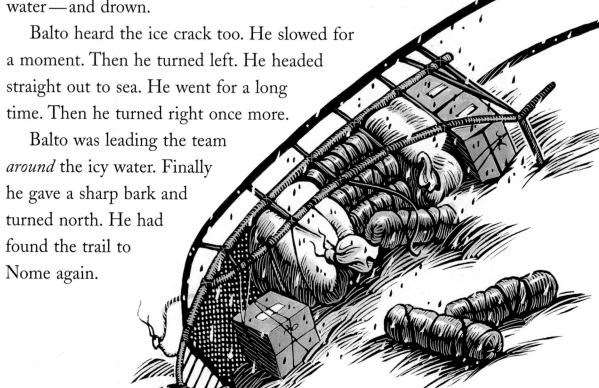

206

Soon the trail left the sea ice. From now on it was over land. Things should have been easier. They weren't. The snow was falling thick and fast. In some places the wind swept most of it off the trail. But in other places the snow drifts came up almost over the dogs' heads. And the wind was blowing harder and harder. It sent bits of icy snow straight into Kasson's eyes. "I might as well have been blind," he said. "I couldn't even *guess* where we were."

And the dogs were so tired! Again and again they tried to stop. They wanted to lie down and go to sleep in the snow. Balto was just as tired. But he would not stop. He kept on pulling—and the other dogs had to follow behind.

Now something else began to worry Gunnar Kasson. They had been traveling for about 14 hours. Surely they should have reached the town of Safety in 14 hours. Kasson went on for another hour. Then he knew. Somehow they had missed the town in the storm. They must have passed right by the new dog team!

Kasson knew they couldn't stop and wait for the storm to die down. He and the dogs would freeze if they did. They couldn't go back to Bluff either. They had come too far. There was only one thing to do now.
Pray . . . and push on to Nome.

Later Gunnar Kasson said he couldn't remember those last miles very well. Each one was a nightmare of howling wind and swirling snow and bitter cold. But somehow—with Balto leading slowly and steadily—they made it! At 5:30 in the morning, February 2, 1925—after 20 hours on the trail—the team limped into Nome!

The whole town was waiting for the medicine! They gathered around Gunnar Kasson. They shook his hand and pounded him on the back. "How can we ever thank you?" one woman cried.

Gunnar Kasson shook his head. Then he sank to his knees beside Balto. He began to pull long splinters of ice from the dog's paws. "Balto, what a dog," he said. "I've been in Alaska for 20 years and this was the toughest trip I've ever made. But Balto, *he* brought us through."

Many newspaper and magazine stories were written about Balto. His picture was printed on postcards and in books. And today, on a grassy hill in New York City's Central Park, there is a life-sized statue of Balto—the dog who saved Nome.

Think About It

1. Describe Gunnar Kasson and Balto's trip. What made the trip dangerous?

2. Why do you think Gunnar and Balto did not give up?

3. How did Balto show that he was a good sled dog and a good leader?

208

Meet the Author
Margaret Davidson

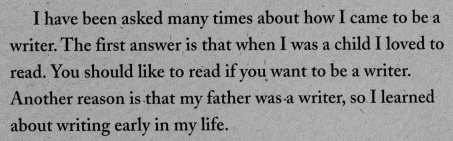

Dear Readers,

   I have been asked many times about how I came to be a writer. The first answer is that when I was a child I loved to read. You should like to read if you want to be a writer. Another reason is that my father was a writer, so I learned about writing early in my life.

   I have written many books and stories. I like writing about famous people such as Thomas Edison, George Washington, and Louis Braille. I like to write about animals, too. Some of my other books have been about dogs, dolphins, and horses.

   I hope you liked reading the exciting story of Balto's adventure in Alaska.

Your friend,

Margaret Davidson

Margaret Davidson

 Visit *The Learning Site!*
www.harcourtschool.com

Sending

Before machines, an important message may have been sent like this:

By a runner

On horseback

By carrier pigeon

From one hilltop to another, by torches, flags, or hand signals

This time line shows some of the ways people have sent important messages. Today you can send a message almost anywhere in the world within minutes or even seconds. It was not always that easy!

1791 First machine is used to send a long-distance message. The arms are moved to show different letters of the alphabet.

1850s–1860s Telegraph lines are strung alongside railroad tracks. Telegraph offices open in every train station.

1790 1800 1810 1820 1830 1840 1850 1860 1870

1837 Samuel Morse invents a telegraph machine. Morse Code is used to tap out a message in dots and dashes.

1866 Telegraph cables under the Atlantic Ocean link North America and Europe.

Atlantic Ocean

a Message

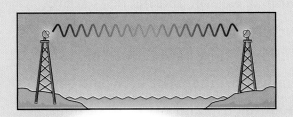

1927 First telephone call across the Atlantic Ocean uses radio waves instead of wires.

1980s Fax machines are used in many offices.

1956 Telephone cables are laid under the Atlantic Ocean.

1880   1890   1900   1910   1920   1930   1940   1950   1960   1970   1980   1990   **2000**

1876 Alexander Graham Bell invents the telephone.

1930s First phototelegraph sends copies of photographs and other pictures.

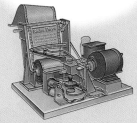

1990s Electronic mail (e-mail) allows people to send a message from one computer to another computer.

Think About It

What kind of information can you find on a time line?

News from Nome

WRITE A POSTCARD

After twenty hours on the trail, Gunnar Kasson and his dogs arrive in Nome. Write a message that Gunnar might have sent to his family. Imagine what he would say about his trip and his team of dogs.

RESPONSE

Alaska Facts

MAKE A FACT BOOK

Did you know that at the beginning of summer, the sun never sets in parts of Alaska? With a group, learn more about this interesting state. Find facts in travel brochures, on an encyclopedia CD-ROM, or on the Internet. Make an Alaskan Facts Book to share.

Balto the Great

MAKE A SIGN

An artist made a statue of Balto to remember what he did. Make a sign to go with the statue. Write some sentences that explain who Balto was and what he and Gunnar Kasson did for the people of Nome, Alaska.

ACTIVITIES

Making Connections

WRITE A PARAGRAPH

Find 1925, the year of Balto's famous journey, on the time line on pages 210–211. Then write a paragraph telling why the people of Nome sent a telegram instead of using another kind of communication.

Little Grunt and

Award-
Winning Author
and Illustrator

the Big Egg

by Tomie dePaola

Once upon a time, in a big cave, past the volcano on the left, lived the Grunt Tribe. There was Unca Grunt, Ant Grunt, Granny Grunt, Mama Grunt, and Papa Grunt. Their leader was Chief Rockhead Grunt. The smallest Grunt of all was Little Grunt.

One Saturday morning, Mama Grunt said to Little Grunt, "Little Grunt, tomorrow the Ugga-Wugga Tribe is coming for Sunday brunch. Could you please go outside and gather two dozen eggs?"

"Yes, Mama Grunt," said Little Grunt, and off he went.

At that time of year, eggs were hard to find. Little Grunt looked and looked. No luck. He was getting tired.

"What am I going to do?" he said to himself. "I can't find a single egg. I'll try one more place."

And it was a good thing that he did, because there, in the one more place, was the biggest egg Little Grunt had ever seen.

It was too big to carry. It was too far to roll. And besides, Little Grunt had to be very careful. Eggs break *very* easily.

Little Grunt thought and thought.

"I know," he said. He gathered some of the thick pointy leaves that were growing nearby. He wove them into a mat. Then he carefully rolled the egg on top of it. He pulled and pulled and pulled the egg all the way home.

"My goodness," said the Grunt Tribe. "Ooga, ooga, what an egg! That will feed us *and* the Ugga-Wuggas. And even the Grizzler Tribe. Maybe we should invite *them* to Sunday brunch, too."

"I'll be able to make that special omelet I've been wanting to," said Mama Grunt.

"Ooga, ooga! Yummy! Yummy!" said all the Grunts.

They put the egg near the hearth, and then they all went to bed.

That night, by the flickering firelight, the egg began to make noise. CLICK, CRACK went the egg. CLICK, CRACK, CLUNK. A big piece fell to the floor. CLICK, CRACK, CLUNK, PLOP. The egg broke in half, and instead of the big egg sitting by the fire . . .

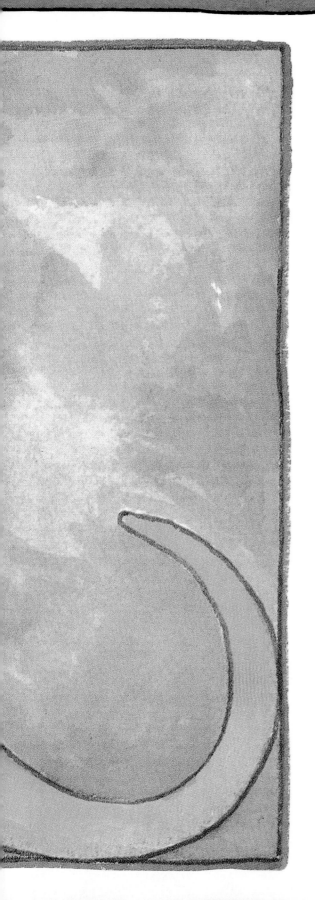

There was a baby dinosaur!

"Waaangh," cried the baby dinosaur. And all the Grunt Tribe woke up.

"Ooga, ooga!" they said. "What are we going to do?"

"There goes the brunch!" said Unca Grunt.

"What will the Ugga-Wuggas say?" said Ant Grunt.

"I bet I'm allergic to that thing," said Papa Grunt.

Chief Rockhead Grunt said, "All I know is it can't stay . . ."

But before he could finish, Little Grunt said, "May I keep him? Please? *Please?*"

"Every boy needs a pet," said Granny Grunt.

Some of the Grunts said yes. Some of the Grunts said no. But it was finally decided that Little Grunt could keep the baby dinosaur.

"Against my better judgment," mumbled Chief Rockhead Grunt.

"Oh, well, I suppose I can make pancakes for Sunday brunch," said Mama Grunt.

"I'm going to call him George," said Little Grunt.

Little Grunt and George became great pals.

But there was a problem. The cave stayed the same size, but George didn't. He began to grow.

And GROW.
And **GROW.**

The cave got very crowded.

And there were other problems. George wasn't housebroken. George ate ALL the leaves off ALL the trees and ALL the bushes ALL around the cave. But still he was hungry. George liked to play—rough. George stepped on things. And when he sneezed—well, it was a disaster.

"Ooga, ooga! Enough is enough!" said the Grunts.

"Either that dinosaur goes, or I go," said Unca Grunt.

"I spend all day getting food for him," said Ant Grunt.

"Achoo!" said Papa Grunt. "I told you I was allergic to him."

"He stepped on all my cooking pots and broke them," said Mama Grunt.

"I guess it wasn't a good idea to keep him," said Granny Grunt. "How about a nice *little* cockroach. They make nice pets."

"I'm in charge here," said Chief Rockhead Grunt. "And I say, *That giant lizard goes!*"

"Ooga, ooga! Yes! Yes!" said all the Grunts.

"But you promised," said Little Grunt.

The next morning, Little Grunt took George away from the cave, out to where he had found him in the first place.

"Good-bye, George," said Little Grunt. "I'll sure miss you."

"Waaargh," said George.

Big tears rolled down both their cheeks. Sadly, Little Grunt watched as George walked slowly into the swamp.

"I'll never see him again," sobbed Little Grunt.

The days and months went by, and Little Grunt still missed George. He dreamed about him at night and drew pictures of him by day.

"Little Grunt certainly misses that dinosaur," said Mama Grunt.

"He'll get over it," said Papa Grunt.

"It's nice and peaceful here again," said Ant and Unca Grunt.

"I still say a cockroach makes a nice pet," said Granny Grunt.

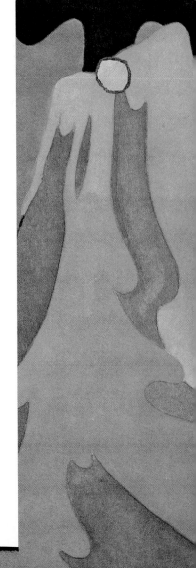

"Ooga, ooga. Torches out. Everyone in bed," said Chief Rockhead.

That night, the cave started to shake. The floor began to pitch, and loud rumblings filled the air.

"Earthquake!" cried the Grunts, and they rushed to the opening of the cave.

"No, it's not," said Granny Grunt. "Look! Volcano!"

And sure enough, the big volcano was erupting all over the place. Steam and rocks and black smoke shot out of the top. Around the cave, big rocks and boulders tumbled and bounced.

"We're trapped! We're trapped!" shouted the Grunts. "What are we going to do?"

"Don't ask me!" said Chief Rockhead. "I resign."

"Now we have no leader," cried Ant Grunt.

"Now we're really in trouble!" shouted Papa Grunt.

The lava was pouring out of the volcano in a wide, flaming river and was heading straight for the cave.

There wasn't enough time for the Grunts to escape. All of a sudden, the Grunts heard a different noise.

"Waaargh! Wonk!"

"It's George," cried Little Grunt. "He's come to save us."

"Ooga, ooga! Quick!" said the Grunts as they all jumped on George's long neck and long back and long tail.

And before you could say Tyrannosaurus rex, George carried them far away to safety.

"As your new leader," Papa Grunt said, "I say this is our new cave!"

"I like the kitchen," said Mama Grunt.

"Now, when I was the leader . . ." said Plain Rockhead Grunt.

"When do we eat?" said Unca Grunt.

"I can't wait to start decorating," said Ant Grunt.

"I always say a change of scenery keeps you from getting old," said Granny Grunt.

"And George can live right next door," said Little Grunt.

"Where is George?" asked Mama Grunt. "I haven't seen him all afternoon."

"Ooga, ooga. Here, George," called the Grunts.

"Waaargh," answered George.

"Look!" said Little Grunt.

"Oh no!" said the Grunts.

There was George, sitting on a pile of big eggs.

"I guess I'd better call George Georgina!" said Little Grunt.

And they all lived happily ever after.

Think About It

1. How do Little Grunt and George work together during the story?

2. Why do you think it is hard for Little Grunt to send George away?

3. How can you tell that the story is not about something that really happened?

Meet the Author and Illustrator
Tomie dePaola

Tomie dePaola has always had a talent for art. Even as a small child, Tomie was good at drawing. "I guess I saw things differently than most of my school friends. . . . I saw with my eyes like everyone else but I also saw 'inside' with 'inner eyes.' My mother told me that was imagination."

Tomie dePaola's other great talent is for telling stories. When he was a boy, there was no television. He listened to stories his mother read aloud, and he learned about storytelling from her. There was also the radio. Every Saturday morning Tomie listened to his favorite show, "Let's Pretend," and let his imagination grow.

Tomie dePaola enjoyed taking art classes in high school and decided to go on to art school. Afterward, he knew he wanted to make children's books, and he showed his work to many publishers. It's hard to believe now that it was six years before he was asked to illustrate a book!

Visit *The Learning Site!* www.harcourtschool.com

A Place of Their Own

from *Contact Kids* magazine

by Carol Pugliano

Popcorn Park Zoo is a very special place for animals. John Bergmann is the zoo's general manager. He and his staff save wild animals who are hurt. They take the animals to Popcorn Park Zoo in Forked River, New Jersey, where they can live and get better.

Popcorn Park wasn't always a zoo. Twenty years ago, it was called the Forked River Animal Care Center. The Center found homes for cats and dogs.

Then along came Rigby the raccoon. One day, Bergmann got a call from a woman who had found a raccoon in her backyard. Its leg was caught in a trap. The animal had dragged itself from the woods to the woman's house.

Bergmann and a man from the New Jersey Humane Society rescued Rigby from the trap. But the raccoon's leg was so badly hurt, its front paw had to be removed.

Without his paw, Rigby couldn't find food or defend himself. So he couldn't be released into the wild. Instead, Bergmann built Rigby a tree house at the Animal Care Center—and the zoo was born!

Out of the Wild

Today, more than 250 animals call the Popcorn Park Zoo home. Almost all of them have a story to tell. There are deer that have been hit by cars and only have three legs. There are pot-bellied pigs that grew too big to be pets. There are bears, lions and other circus animals that have been treated badly.

Many zoo residents, like Cindy Lou the cougar, are wild animals that people found and kept. Thinking she could be raised like a pet, Cindy Lou's owners had her teeth filed down and her claws removed. But the owners soon realized that wild animals aren't meant to be pets. They wanted to get rid of Cindy Lou. But she couldn't be returned to the wild. Popcorn Park Zoo gave Cindy Lou a second chance at a happy life.

Other residents are wild animals that have been hurt. Bergmann and the zoo's staff take care of these animals. Most of them become well enough to be released back into the wild. That's Bergmann's favorite part about working at the zoo. "There's nothing better than seeing the white tail of a deer as it runs back into the woods," he told *Contact Kids*. "It's a really good feeling."

Think About It

How does Popcorn Park Zoo help animals?

235

Life with George

WRITE A STORY

Imagine what might have happened if the Grunt family had kept George. Write a short story about what life with George might have been like for the Grunts. Share your story with a classmate.

Response

Rock Painting

DRAW A STORY SCENE

Little Grunt makes rock paintings of the dinosaur. Make your own rock painting. Crumple up a brown paper bag, and then lay it flat. Draw a picture showing your favorite part of the story. Write a sentence that tells why you like this part of the story.

Volcano!

DRAW A DIAGRAM

When a volcano erupts, lava, rocks, and gas shoot out. Look for information in an encyclopedia or in a book about volcanoes. Find out what a volcano looks like on the inside. Draw a picture that shows the different parts of a volcano. Label the parts.

Activities

Making Connections

WRITE ABOUT AN OPINION

The author of "A Place of Their Own" says that wild animals aren't meant to be pets. Do you agree with this? Write a paragraph telling what you think and why. Use examples from "Little Grunt and the Big Egg" and from "A Place of Their Own."

Theme

What I Liked Best

EXPRESS VIEWPOINTS   Look through the selection you liked best in this theme to find your favorite sentence or scene. Write a few sentences to tell why you liked the sentence or scene. Then answer the questions below.

- Which animal did you most like reading about? Why?

- Which character in the story would you most like to meet? Tell why.

Agree or Disagree?

DEBATE STATEMENTS   Read each statement below, and think about the stories, articles, and poems you have read. Decide whether you agree or disagree with the statement. Give reasons, using examples from the selections.

"People and animals don't work well together."

"People should sometimes allow animals to lead the way."

"Wild animals need people's help."

Wrap-Up

Set the Stage

CREATE A DRAMATIC SCENE   With a group of students, choose from one selection a scene that shows animals and people helping one another. One group member can read the scene aloud while the rest pretend to be the story characters, "frozen" in the scene. Present the scene to classmates.

CONTENTS

THEME

Friends Grow

to
With

Reader's Choice

Ramona Quimby, Age 8

by Beverly Cleary

REALISTIC FICTION/NOVEL

Ramona works hard to get her family through hard times.

Newbery Honor; ALA Notable Book; Children's Choice

READER'S CHOICE LIBRARY

Making Friends

by Sarah Levete

NONFICTION

Children share what they have learned and how they feel about making and keeping friends.

READER'S CHOICE LIBRARY

Back Home
by Gloria Jean Pinkney

HISTORICAL FICTION

A city girl from the North learns about farm life in the South when she visits her mother's relatives.

ALA Notable Book; Notable Trade Book in Social Studies

Lester's Dog
by Karen Hesse

REALISTIC FICTION

Together, two boys find the courage to face the neighbor's dog.

SLJ **Best Book; Notable Trade Book in Social Studies**

Tomás and the Library Lady
by Pat Mora

BIOGRAPHY

His grandfather and a librarian help Tomás find adventure in books.

Teachers' Choice

The Stories Julian Tells

by Ann Cameron

Illustrated by Cornelius Van Wright
and Ying-Hwa Hu

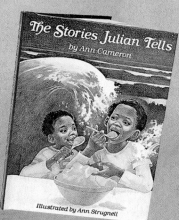

Gloria, Who Might Be My Best Friend

If you have a girl for a friend, people find out and tease you. That's why I didn't want a girl for a friend— not until this summer, when I met Gloria.

It happened one afternoon when I was walking down the street by myself. My mother was visiting a friend of hers, and Huey was visiting a friend of his. Huey's friend is five and so I think he is too young to play with. And there aren't any kids just my age. I was walking down the street feeling lonely.

A block from our house I saw a moving van in front of a brown house, and men were carrying in chairs and tables and bookcases and boxes full of I don't know what. I watched for a while, and suddenly I heard a voice right behind me.

"Who are you?"

I turned around and there was a girl in a yellow dress. She looked the same age as me. She had curly hair that was braided into two pigtails with red ribbons at the ends.

"I'm Julian," I said. "Who are you?"

"I'm Gloria," she said. "I come from Newport. Do you know where Newport is?"

I wasn't sure, but I didn't tell Gloria. "It's a town on the ocean," I said.

"Right," Gloria said. "Can you turn a cartwheel?"

She turned sideways herself and did two cartwheels on the grass.

I had never tried a cartwheel before, but I tried to copy Gloria. My hands went down in the grass, my feet went up in the air, and—I fell over.

I looked at Gloria to see if she was laughing at me. If she was laughing at me, I was going to go home and forget about her.

But she just looked at me very seriously and said, "It takes practice," and then I liked her.

"I know where there's a bird's nest in your yard," I said.

"Really?" Gloria said. "There weren't any trees in the yard, or any birds, where I lived before."

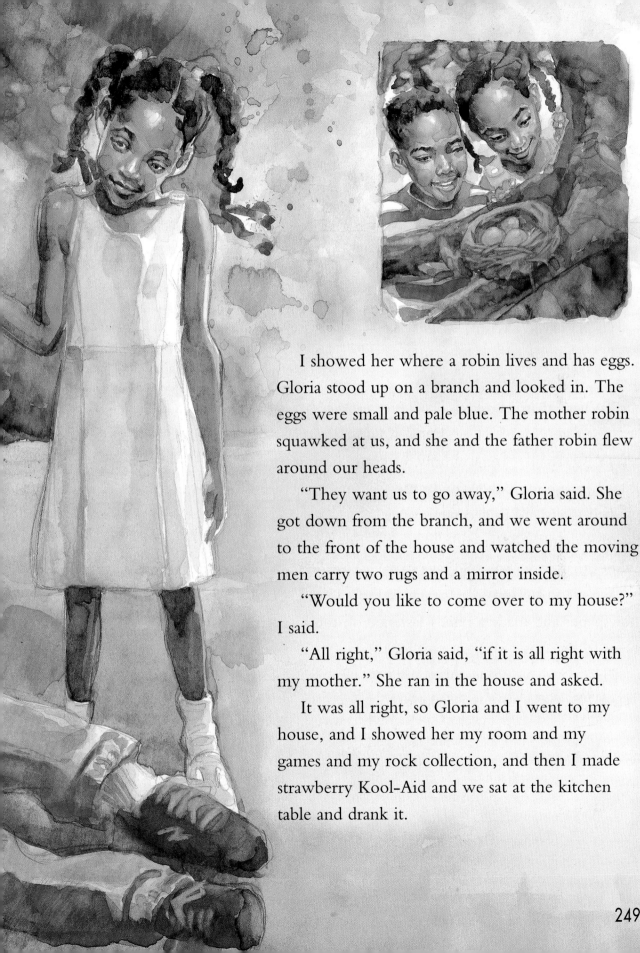

I showed her where a robin lives and has eggs.
Gloria stood up on a branch and looked in. The
eggs were small and pale blue. The mother robin
squawked at us, and she and the father robin flew
around our heads.

"They want us to go away," Gloria said. She
got down from the branch, and we went around
to the front of the house and watched the moving
men carry two rugs and a mirror inside.

"Would you like to come over to my house?"
I said.

"All right," Gloria said, "if it is all right with
my mother." She ran in the house and asked.

It was all right, so Gloria and I went to my
house, and I showed her my room and my
games and my rock collection, and then I made
strawberry Kool-Aid and we sat at the kitchen
table and drank it.

"You have a red mustache on your mouth," Gloria said.

"You have a red mustache on your mouth, too," I said.

Gloria giggled, and we licked off the mustaches with our tongues.

"I wish you'd live here a long time," I told Gloria.

Gloria said, "I wish I would too."

"I know the best way to make wishes," Gloria said.

"What's that?" I asked.

"First you make a kite. Do you know how to make one?"

"Yes," I said, "I know how." I know how to make good kites because my father taught me. We make them out of two crossed sticks and folded newspaper.

"All right," Gloria said, "that's the first part of making wishes that come true. So let's make a kite."

We went out into the garage and spread out sticks and newspaper and made a kite. I fastened on the kite string and went to the closet and got rags for the tail.

"Do you have some paper and two pencils?" Gloria asked. "Because now we make the wishes."

I didn't know what she was planning, but I went in the house and got pencils and paper.

"All right," Gloria said. "Every wish you want to have come true you write on a long thin piece of paper. You don't tell me your wishes, and I don't tell you mine. If you tell, your wishes don't come true. Also, if you look at the other person's wishes, your wishes don't come true."

Gloria sat down on the garage floor again and started writing her wishes. I wanted to see what they were — but I went to the other side of the garage and wrote my own wishes instead. I wrote:

1. I wish I could see the catalog cats.

2. I wish the fig tree would be the tallest in town.

3. I wish I'd be a great soccer player.

4. I wish I could ride in an airplane.

5. I wish Gloria would stay here and be my best friend.

253

I folded my five wishes in my fist and went over to Gloria.

"How many wishes did you make?" Gloria asked.

"Five," I said. "How many did you make?"

"Two," Gloria said.

I wondered what they were.

"Now we put the wishes on the tail of the kite," Gloria said. "Every time we tie one piece of rag on the tail, we fasten a wish in the knot. You can put yours in first."

I fastened mine in, and then Gloria fastened in hers, and we carried the kite into the yard.

"You hold the tail," I told Gloria, "and I'll pull."

We ran through the back yard with the kite, passed the garden and the fig tree, and went into the open field beyond our yard.

The kite started to rise. The tail jerked heavily like a long white snake. In a minute the kite passed the roof of my house and was climbing toward the sun.

We stood in the open field, looking up at it. I was wishing I would get my wishes.

"I know it's going to work!" Gloria said.

"How do you know?"

"When we take the kite down," Gloria told me, "there shouldn't be one wish in the tail. When the wind takes all your wishes, that's when you know it's going to work." The kite stayed up for a long time. We both held the string.

The kite looked like a tiny black spot in the sun, and my neck got stiff from looking at it.

"Shall we pull it in?" I asked.

"All right," Gloria said.

We drew the string in more and more until, like a tired bird, the kite fell at our feet.

We looked at the tail. All our wishes were gone. Probably they were still flying higher and higher in the wind.

Maybe I would see the catalog cats and get to be a good soccer player and have a ride in an airplane and the tallest fig tree in town. And Gloria would be my best friend.

"Gloria," I said, "did you wish we would be friends?"

"You're not supposed to ask me that!" Gloria said.

"I'm sorry," I answered. But inside I was smiling. I guessed one thing Gloria wished for. I was pretty sure we would be friends.

THINK ABOUT IT

1 Describe the main characters Gloria and Julian, using examples from the story.

2 Will Gloria be a good friend for Julian? Give reasons for your answer.

3 If you made this story into a TV program, what three places would you need to show?

Meet the Author
Ann Cameron

Question: Who was your best friend when you were growing up?

Ann Cameron: My best friend was a boy named Bradley. I got teased about him because we were together a lot.

Question: So a boy was your best friend, and you were teased about this. Why did you decide to have Gloria as Julian's best friend?

Ann Cameron: I had a friend from South Africa, Julian, who told me about his childhood—the kite that he flew; his brother, Huey; and his best friend, Gloria. I thought it was neat that Julian's best friend had been a girl. I never thought of leaving her out of the stories.

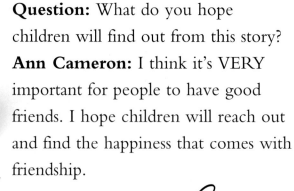

Question: What do you hope children will find out from this story?

Ann Cameron: I think it's VERY important for people to have good friends. I hope children will reach out and find the happiness that comes with friendship.

Ann Cameron

Visit *The Learning Site!*
www.harcourtschool.com

Meet the Illustrators
Cornelius Van Wright and Ying-Hwa Hu

Question: How long have you been working as a team?

Ying-Hwa Hu: We have been working together since 1989.

Question: How many projects have you worked on?

Ying-Hwa Hu: We have done fifteen picture books together. We have both worked on other books separately.

Question: How do you split up the work on a book you illustrate together?

Cornelius Van Wright: Usually, I work out with the publisher what will be pictured on each page. Together, Ying-Hwa and I work on the look of the people. Both of us do some of the drawing. We try to work with each other's strengths. When we paint, one starts and passes it to the other.

RESPONSE

WRITE A LETTER

Julian learns a lot from his friendship with Gloria. Think about what Julian has learned. Then imagine that Julian has gotten a letter from someone who does not believe boys and girls can be friends. Write a letter that Julian might send back to that person.

MAKE A BOOKLET

Julian helps Gloria feel at home in her neighborhood. Make a booklet that would help someone your age get to know your neighborhood. Include a map of nearby streets. Tell where to find the best ice cream, the best park, or other things someone new might want to know.

ACTIVITIES

WRITE INSTRUCTIONS

Julian shows Gloria how to make a kite. Think of something you can do. You may know how to make a sandwich, set the table, or make a greeting card. Write instructions for a younger student. What things will he or she need? What is the first step? Make sure your instructions are clear.

WRITE A POEM

Julian and Gloria both enjoy flying kites. Think about how they may feel when they take the kite outside, or when the kite is finally high above them. How would they describe what they see, smell, and feel? Write a poem that one of them might write.

Synonyms and Antonyms

In "The Stories Julian Tells," the author describes flying a kite.

> The kite started to rise. The tail jerked heavily like a long white snake. In a minute the kite passed the roof of my house and was climbing toward the sun.

Authors carefully choose words to describe people, places, and actions. They sometimes use synonyms and antonyms. **Synonyms** are words that have almost the same meaning. **Antonyms** are words that have opposite, or nearly opposite, meanings. A thesaurus or synonym finder can help you find synonyms for words you meet in stories. This diagram shows how synonyms and antonyms are related.

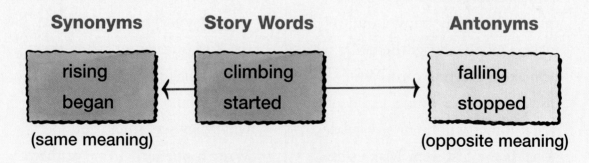

Synonyms	Story Words	Antonyms
rising began	← climbing started →	falling stopped
(same meaning)		(opposite meaning)

Knowing about synonyms and antonyms can help you understand new words. If you are not sure about the meaning of a word, you can reread or read ahead to find synonyms or antonyms to use as clues. Read the following paragraph, and look for synonyms or antonyms for the underlined words.

Kim moved from a country farm to an <u>urban</u> neighborhood. There are <u>several</u> apartments in her building. Kim has met many of her neighbors. She loves the <u>bustling</u> city streets, as well as the peaceful, green park nearby.

WHAT HAVE YOU LEARNED?

1. What would happen to a sentence if you changed a word to its antonym?

2. Give a synonym for the underlined word:
Julian <u>yelled</u>, "The kite is stuck in a tree!"

TRY THIS ● TRY THIS ● TRY THIS

Choose a paragraph from a library book or a textbook. In a diagram, write some of the action words from the paragraph. Then write some synonyms and antonyms for each word.

Visit *The Learning Site!*
www.harcourtschool.com

263

The Talent Show

by Susan Wojciechowski
illustrated by Laura Ovresat

Ms. Babbitt came to school one morning wearing her smiley face earrings, the ones that mean something special is going to happen. Kelsey asked her why she was wearing them. But Ms. Babbitt said she wouldn't tell till the end of the day.

Right before dismissal Ms. Babbitt said, "Boys and girls, I have something special to announce. Two weeks from today this class is going to have a talent show. It'll be in the gym, and all the first, second, and third graders will come to see it. We won't have winners. We won't have prizes. It's just going to be for fun. You may perform anything you'd like—a poem, a song, a joke, a dance. Are there any questions?"

Carol Ann asked, "Can we wear costumes?"

"You may wear costumes or not, whichever you prefer."

Steven asked, "Can we do stuff in groups?"

"You may perform alone or in groups."

Pam asked, "If we say a poem, do we have to rememberize it, or can we read it off a paper?"

"I think it would be much more effective if you memorized it."

Leo asked, "Can I have my dog in my act?"

"You may, but someone must bring the dog at the time of the show. It may not roam around our classroom all day distracting the class."

Wendy, who's shy and talks so quietly you can hardly hear her, asked, "Do we have to do something?"

"No one has to be in the show, but I think those of you who choose to be a part of it will have lots of fun."

The dismissal bell rang and we all ran for the buses, talking about the talent show.

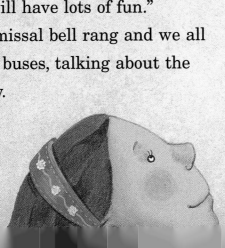

That night, Carol Ann called me on the phone. "Beany, I have the greatest idea for the talent show. You and I are going to recite a poem together. I wrote a poem that has lines for two people to say. It's about bees—a queen bee and a worker bee. It'll be the best act in the whole show. If they gave awards, this act would win first place. We'll practice every day after school. My mother will make the costumes. You'll be the worker bee and I'll be the queen bee."

"Why do you get to be the queen?" I asked.

"Because I have curly hair, silly. Don't you know anything?"

The next day Carol Ann gave me a copy of the poem. We practiced at her house after school. Carol Ann stretched out on big pillows to say her lines. I had to stand holding a mop and a pail. Carol Ann said those were props and they made us look our parts.

I didn't want to hold a pail and mop while Carol Ann lay on pillows, but I didn't complain because, number one, Carol Ann is very bossy and I'm a tiny bit scared of her and, number two, I didn't have any better ideas for an act.

The day after that we practiced at my house. Carol Ann wore a crown. I didn't.

On Saturday Carol Ann decided I should say my lines in a low, growly voice like a worker who is tired and she should say her lines soft and tinkly like a queen.

On Monday Carol Ann showed me pictures she drew of the costumes. Carol Ann's had a gold ruffled ballerina skirt. Mine had a big black-and-yellow-striped T-shirt and black tights.

A week before the show Carol Ann said, "Let's talk about all the things that might go wrong."

"Let's not," I said.

Carol Ann ignored that and started to list them: "I'm worried you might forget your lines, or drop your mop, or get a run in your tights, or trip over your pail, or get the hiccups, or sneeze."

That's when I started to worry. I worried that I would spit when I talked. I worried that my antennae would fall down over my face. I worried that instead of saying, "I feed the queen and build the hive," I would say, "I feed the hive and build the queen."

Every night at supper I said my lines to my family. Every night in bed I bit my nails thinking about doing the bee poem.

268

One night as I was repeating, "I feed the queen and build the hive," over and over during supper, my dad said, "Beany, relax. You're supposed to be enjoying this talent show."

"I know. Ms. Babbitt even said the show was for fun. But I'm not having any. I know I'll do something wrong and Carol Ann will be mad at me."

"Then why are you doing an act with her?" my brother asked.

"It just sort of happened. Besides, I don't have any better ideas."

"How about doing the cartwheels you just learned in gymnastics class?" my mother asked. "Your teacher said you do them really well."

"Carol Ann wouldn't like that. She's got everything all figured out for us."

That night as I lay in bed biting my nails, my dad tiptoed into my room.

"Are you awake?" he whispered.

"I can't sleep," I said. "I'm thinking about the bee poem."

"I want to show you something wonderful," Dad said. He swung me and Jingle Bell onto his back and carried us down the stairs and out the front door. There were two sleeping bags spread out on the driveway. Jingle Bell and I lay on top of one of them and Dad lay on the other.

"Look at the sky," he said. "I don't think I've ever seen it so beautiful. I wanted to share it with you."

Dad was right. The sky looked like black ink. The stars looked like white polka dots.

"How many stars are there?" I asked my dad.

"Billions," he answered.

"I mean, what's the exact number?"

"That's a mystery."

"I'm going to count them," I decided. So I picked a spot to start at and tried to keep track of which stars I had counted and which ones were left. When I got to twenty-seven, I got mixed up and had to start over. This time I got to thirty-two before I got mixed up again. I started a third time.

Dad stopped me. "You know something, Beany? I don't think you should count the stars. There are some things in life that are just meant to be enjoyed."

"You mean like a dish of double chocolate ice cream with colored sprinkles and whipped cream on top?" I asked.

"Yes," he said, "and like a sausage, pepperoni, and onion pizza."

"And like kittens," I added.

"Right. And like Beethoven's Fifth Symphony."

"And like a starry, starry night, Daddy?"

"Yes, like a starry, starry night."

We looked up at the sky for a while. Then my dad asked, "Do you know what else should just be enjoyed?"

"What?"

"A talent show."

He reached over to my sleeping bag and squeezed my hand. We lay there looking up at the stars for a long time. Not counting them. Just enjoying them.

The next day on the bus ride to school I took a deep breath and said to Carol Ann, "I don't want to do the bee poem. I want to do cartwheels across the gym floor."

"Why?" she asked.

"Because cartwheels are fun."

"What would you wear?"

"Shorts and a T-shirt."

"What kind of music would you have?"

"No music."

"How many cartwheels would you do?"

"As many as it takes."

"What if you fall?"

"I'll get up and keep going."

"What if you do a cartwheel into Kevin Gates?"

"Carol Ann, quit it," I said. "I'm doing cartwheels no matter what you say." Then I gave her back the paper with my bee poem lines.

On Friday our class put on the best talent show in the whole world. For his talent, Boomer Fenton showed his birthmark in the shape of a dog's face. Kelsey played "Twinkle, Twinkle, Little Star" on her violin. Leo tried to get his dog to roll over, but the dog ran under Ms. Babbitt's chair and wouldn't come out for the rest of the show. Carol Ann and Wendy did the bee poem. Carol Ann's crown fell off right in the middle of it.

For my talent, I did cartwheels from one end of the gym to the other. It was fun.

Think About It

1 Why doesn't Beany want to be in the talent show with Carol Ann?

2 What is Beany's father like? How do you know?

3 Do you think Beany shows courage in this story? Explain why you think as you do.

Meet the Author
Susan Wojciechowski

A few years ago Susan Wojciechowski had the flu. While she was lying in bed, the idea for a story character, Beany, popped into her head. "Beany just stayed there, and by the time I was well, the stories were written," she said.

Susan Wojciechowski wasn't always a writer. First, she was a school teacher. Later, she worked as a school librarian. She is also the mother of three children.

Her books include stories for teenagers as well as picture books for young readers. She hopes that her readers see her characters as real people and that they see a little of themselves in the character Beany.

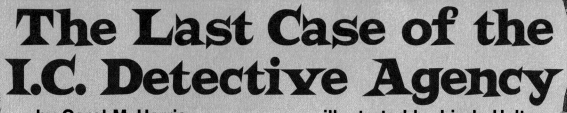

The Last Case of the I.C. Detective Agency

by Carol M. Harris   **illustrated by Linda Helton**

"Hey!" Ivan's little brother, Ben, yelled. "The new people are pulling up. I see a kid."

Ivan didn't care if twenty kids moved into Apartment 2A where his friend Charlie used to live. Nobody could replace Charlie. It was Charlie who had started the I.C. Detective Agency (*I* for Ivan, *C* for Charlie). It was Charlie who had thought of all the good ideas and found all the good cases. Now that he had moved away, there would be no detective agency, no cases, and no fun.

For two whole days Ivan managed to avoid the new kid in 2A. "Her name is Ursula, and she's going to be in your class," his little brother told him. "She says she wants to be friends with you."

Ivan didn't want to be friends with her. But one day she came right up to him while he was sitting on the front steps, and she said, "Hi. Ben told me you have a detective agency."

"Well, I don't," Ivan mumbled. He started to leave.

"That's too bad," she said with a frown. "I need a detective."

He stared at her. "What for?"

"Why should I tell you if you're not a detective? I'll figure it out myself." She started down the stairs.

"Wait! Figure what out?"

She took a crumpled paper out of her pocket and shoved it at him. "What does this mean?"

Ivan smoothed out the paper and read the words printed on it:

"Where did this come from?" he asked, staring at Ursula.

"It was between the window and the screen in my bedroom," she answered. "Spooky, huh? It looks like code. I think spies lived in our apartment before we moved in."

5OOK UND74 T27 4UG.1234567

"Charlie lived there, dopey," Ivan said.

"Maybe he was a spy."

"He wasn't a spy, dopey. He was my partner in the I.C. Detective Agency."

"Well, he couldn't have been a very good detective if he didn't see this note," Ursula said, pulling it away from him. "And stop calling me 'dopey'!"

"I'm sorry," Ivan said quickly. "I'll help you."

He knew it wouldn't be the same as working on a case with Charlie, but it was better than nothing.

"Do you want to take a look at the crime scene?" Ursula asked.

Ivan's eyes widened. She knew detective talk.

It was strange seeing Ursula's mother instead of Charlie's in Apartment 2A, and it was even stranger to be working on a case in the room where he and his friend had solved so many mysteries together. Ursula pointed out the spot where she'd found the note, then sat down at her desk.

"Here," she said, handing Ivan a paper and pencil. "Let's get to work."

"We have to find the code breaker," Ivan said, bending his head over the paper. "1234567 has to be it. We've got to figure out what that word is."

"You mean the numbers stand for letters?" Ursula asked.

"Sure. At least that's how most codes work," he explained. "They substitute a number for each letter of the alphabet, like 1 for *A* and 2 for *B*, and 3 for *C*. Charlie and I used that code sometimes."

But when Ivan and Ursula tried it on the note, it didn't work. "It doesn't make sense," said Ursula, looking over his shoulder.

"I know." Ivan scratched his head. "I wish Charlie were here," he muttered. "We'd work it out in no time."

500K UND74 T27 4UG. 1234567
EOOK UNDGD TBG DUG. ABCDEFG

Ursula looked up. "Hey!" she said suddenly. "Was this Charlie's room?"

"Yeah. So?"

She didn't answer but started scribbling furiously. "That's it," she yelled. Then she ran to each corner of the room and tugged at the edges of the rug.

Ivan watched with a puzzled expression as she bent down and pulled up a loose corner of the rug.

"Bingo!" Triumphantly she held up a second note. She read it quickly. Dancing across the room, she handed the first note to Ivan. "Read this," she ordered.

"Charlie?" Ivan wrinkled his forehead.

500K UND74 T27 4UG. 1234567
~~EOOK UNDGD TBG DUG. ABCDEFG~~
LOOK UNDER THE RUG. CHARLIE

"Your friend Charlie left that note," Ursula said, laughing. "He used his own name for the code breaker."

"I don't believe it," Ivan said.

She handed him the second note. "Read it out loud."

Ivan read:

TO WHOEVER FINDS THIS NOTE:

You passed the test. You cracked the code. Ask Ivan if you can be in the I.C. Detective Agency. He needs a new partner.

Charlie (code breaker 1234567)

"Boy, leave it to Charlie to do something like this!" Ivan said.

"Well?" Ursula asked. "Can I be in the I.C. Detective Agency?"

Ivan shook his head. "No."

She frowned. "But didn't Charlie's note say . . ."

Ivan laughed. "I think we need a new name," he said. "How about the I.C.U. Detective Agency?"

"I get it," Ursula said. "*I* for Ivan, *C* for Charlie, and *U* for Ursula."

"Right! You're a great detective!"

"I know," she said with a grin. "I think our first case should be to send a letter to Charlie. In code!"

Ivan grinned back. They started writing. "Let's see if Charlie can figure that out, partner," said Ivan.

Ivan (code breaker 1234) and Ursula (code breaker 567583) shook hands.

DE36 CH3681E,
WE J57T 7082ED THE
837T C37E OF THE 1.C.
DETECT12E 3GE4CY.
F6OM
1234 & 567583
THE 1.C.5.
DETECT12E 3GE4CY

Think About It

How do Ivan's feelings change from the beginning to the end of the story?

Response

A Poem for Two

WRITE A POEM

Carol Ann wrote a poem about a queen bee and a worker bee. Think of two creatures or two people that go together in an interesting way. Write a poem about the pair. With a partner, read your poem aloud to some classmates.

Making Connections

WRITE IN CODE

Ivan and Beany each learn important lessons about sharing talents and interests with friends. Think of a lesson you have learned about friendship. Write it in one sentence. Then rewrite it in code. Use your own name as a code breaker. Give your coded message to a classmate to solve.

Activities

Talent Show

PERFORM A SKIT

With a small group, write a script for a short skit based on the story "The Talent Show." Choose roles, and perform your skit for classmates.

Talent Show Critic

REVIEW A SHOW

Imagine you are a reporter for Beany's school newspaper. Write a review of the talent show put on by Ms. Babbitt's class. Tell what each performer did and what you liked about his or her act. Give reasons for your opinions.

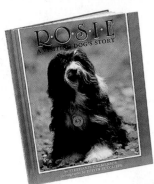

ROSIE
A VISITING DOG'S STORY

Award-Winning
Author

by Stephanie Calmenson
photographs by Justin Sutcliffe

This is Rosie, my dog. She loves to play
fetch. She will roll over to have her belly
rubbed. And she will lick you on the
nose if you are her friend.

Rosie is like many other dogs—maybe even like
your dog. But in one way, Rosie is special.

287

Rosie is a working dog. Here she is in her uniform. Her red harness and special badges say to everyone, *I am a visiting dog.* A visiting dog's job is to cheer up people who are sad, or sick, or lonely.

Rosie was not always a visiting dog. She had to be trained for her work.

This is how Rosie looked when she was a puppy. You could see her eyes! Rosie the puppy would not have been a good visiting dog. She was too wild and silly.

Rosie liked to snoop. Rosie left puddles in all the wrong places. Rosie chewed everything in sight!

But even as a puppy Rosie was gentle and friendly. And she was a good listener. I knew that Rosie would make a good visiting dog someday.

We started Rosie's training at puppy kindergarten. Robin Kovary was our teacher. She taught me how to teach Rosie.

Robin was firm but always gentle. That was important because Rosie had to trust people. She had to be confident that no one would harm her. Rosie also needed to keep her independent spirit. She might have to make a decision on her own while working one day.

Rosie liked school. She learned her lessons fast.

Rosie, sit. Good dog!

Rosie, down. Good dog!

Rosie, stay. Good dog!

Rosie, come. Good dog!

At home, I tried to prepare Rosie for her work. First, it was important for Rosie to be a happy dog. After all, a sad dog could not cheer anyone up. So we played a lot of games. Her favorites were fetch and "catch-me-if-you-can."

Rosie would also have to get along with other dogs in case she had to work alongside them. So she got plenty of time to play with her friends.

A good visiting dog has to be comfortable with all kinds of people. I introduced Rosie to as many different people as I could.

On one street Rosie would sit quietly with an elderly person.

On the next street she would run and play with a child.

Rosie always had good sense. If a person wanted to play, Rosie played. If a person seemed shy, Rosie would lie down and wait for the person to come to her.

Rosie was ready to join a visiting dog program at the ASPCA[1] when she was two years old. Her real training was about to begin.

Our teacher was Micky Niego. In the class there were big dogs and small dogs, short-haired and long-haired dogs, pedigrees and mixed breeds.

All the dogs had two things in common: They were friendly and they were happy to work.

Micky began the class by having the dogs practice their basic obedience skills: Sit, down, stay, come. Then Micky added new skills.

---

[1]ASPCA: American Society for the Prevention of Cruelty to Animals

Rosie learned to "Go say hello." This means that Rosie will not approach a person until she is told that the person is ready to greet her.

She learned the "Don't touch" command. When Rosie hears it she will not touch food or anything else until she hears, "Okay, take it!" It is important for Rosie never to be rude and grab from a person.

The people Rosie would visit might be using wheelchairs and walkers. So Rosie had to be comfortable with all kinds of equipment.

Rosie also had to get used to being handled in different ways. A young child might pull her tail or her long hair, not knowing any better.

An elderly or ill person might pet her too roughly by mistake.

Rosie had to be patient and gentle even at times like these.

Rosie also had to be a good traveler. To get to work, Rosie might need to ride on a train, a bus, or even an airplane. Rosie was given a special travel pass, which allows her to ride with me.

We took many trips together. Rosie learned to be a quiet, well-mannered traveler. And, of course, she made lots of friends.

After four months of training, Rosie and her classmates were tested. Rosie went into a room with volunteers. The volunteers behaved the way the people Rosie would visit might behave.

A little girl with tubes was on a bed. Rosie did not nip at the tubes the way she would have when she was a puppy. Rosie lay quietly by the little girl's side.

A woman dropped a walker in front of Rosie. Rosie did not bark or snap or act fearful. She calmly stepped out of the way.

There were many tests. Rosie passed them all with flying colors!

A few weeks later, Rosie's badges came in the mail. It was time for our first visit. We were invited to a children's hospital.

Before we went, I took Rosie to her vet, Dr. Jimmy Corrao, for a checkup. A visiting dog has to be healthy.

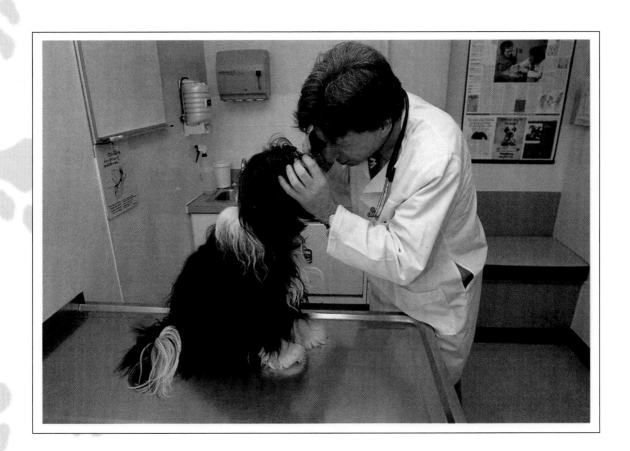

Then I gave Rosie a bath in a special shampoo that made her feel soft and smell sweet.

On the day of our visit, I packed water for Rosie to drink, a soft brush in case someone wanted to groom her, a ball so she could play, and Cheerios to eat.

When we went outside, Rosie had on her red harness, her badges, and a big red bow. I could see that Rosie was proud. She held her head up high.

At the children's hospital, David James, the program director, was waiting for us. I introduced myself and then Rosie.

"Rosie, sit. Paw, please," I said.

Rosie gave Mr. James her paw.

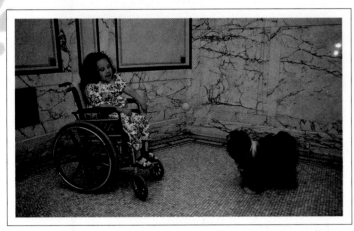

"Hello, Rosie," said Mr. James. "I have some friends I want you to meet. Follow me."

Rosie made a lot of new friends that day. Nina is in a wheelchair because she cannot use her legs. But she has a great throwing arm.

"Rosie, fetch!" she called. Nina threw the ball way across the room. Lucky Rosie! She loves to fetch.

Peter, who is blind, carefully brushed Rosie's long coat.

"Rosie would like to say thank you," I told him.

I turned to Rosie and said, "Speak!" Rosie barked twice to thank Peter for grooming her so well.

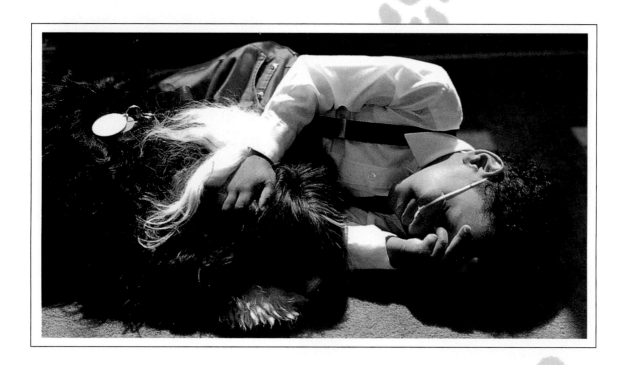

In the next room we met Alexander. Alexander was by himself because he was too sick that day to play with other children. Rosie loved Alexander right away.

The first thing she did was roll over on her back, so Alexander could rub her belly. That made Alexander laugh.

"Rosie looks like a shaggy rug!" he said.

Then Alexander lay down beside Rosie and they napped together awhile.

When they woke up, they shared some Cheerios. I told Alexander how to keep Rosie from grabbing them.

"Rosie, don't touch!" said Alexander.

Rosie turned her head away.

"Okay, take them!" Alexander said.

Rosie ate the Cheerios from Alexander's hand. Then she licked Alexander on the cheek and got a big hug in return.

A few weeks later a call came from The Village Nursing Home asking if Rosie would like to come and visit. We set up an appointment for the next afternoon.

Bea was the first person we met. Bea cannot use her arms or legs, and she has no feeling in them. Bea likes to watch Rosie and to feel Rosie's soft fur against her face.

Then we met Thomas. Thomas was in a wheelchair. Rosie made herself at home in his lap.

"She's cuddly, just like my grandson!" said Thomas.

Down the hall, we heard a woman crying.

"I have so many problems," she said.

"Maybe you'll feel better if you tell them to Rosie," I suggested. "Rosie is a very good listener."

"Rosie?" she asked. She wiped away her tears and started to smile. "My name is Rosie, too!"

The two Rosies had a good visit. Then Linda, a nurse, asked us to look in on Bill down the hall.

"Don't worry if he won't talk to you. He hasn't spoken to anyone in weeks. And he hardly eats. I think he's very lonely," she explained.

I brought Rosie to Bill's room.

"Would you like a visitor?" I asked.

Bill looked at Rosie, then turned away. But then he turned back. For a few minutes he just stared.

Finally he asked in a very quiet voice, "How can the little dog see?"

I told Bill how Rosie's long lashes hold up her hair to let her see through. Suddenly Bill was ready to visit. He had a lot to say about dogs with long hair, and the dog he had when he was a child, and how he wished he had his dog for company now.

I told Bill that Rosie would come visit him again soon. By the time we left, Bill did not seem so lonely anymore. He was saying to Linda, "My dog, Harley, loved to eat cherry Jell-O. Are we having Jell-O for dessert tonight?"

Linda was so happy, she said, "You will have Jell-O if I have to make it for you myself!"

When we left the nursing home, Rosie's tail was way up high and wagging. I offered her a drink of cool water. Then I lifted up her hair to look in her eyes. They were clear and bright.

"Rosie, you are a very good visiting dog," I said. "You are a very good friend."

Think About It

1. What makes Rosie a good visiting dog?

2. If Rosie were a person, what would she be like?

3. What have you learned from Rosie about friendship?

Stephanie Calmenson

Author and Her Dog Cheer Many

Stephanie Calmenson is the author of many books for children. She is also the owner of a six-year-old Tibetan terrier named Rosie. She has trained Rosie to visit sick or lonely people in hospitals and nursing homes in New York City.

When asked why she brings Rosie on these visits, Stephanie Calmenson said, "Ever since I was a little girl living in Brooklyn, I wanted a dog, but I couldn't have one. When I grew up, I got Rosie. She turned out to be so sweet, I wanted to share her with as many people as I could. That is why we joined the visiting dog program."

Before she became a writer, Stephanie Calmenson was a teacher and then an editor for a children's book publisher. The first story she wrote was printed in a magazine. Many people liked her story. Their praise encouraged her to keep on writing.

Visit *The Learning Site!*
www.harcourtschool.com

RESPONSE

Working Dogs

COMPARE CHARACTERS

Compare Rosie to Gloria, Officer Buckle's dog, or to Balto, the dog who saved Nome. Think of words to describe each animal and the work that character does to help humans. Show your ideas in a chart or diagram.

A Portrait of Rosie

WRITE A SHAPE POEM

Choose some words that the author uses to describe Rosie, such as *gentle*, *friendly*, and *shaggy*. Add some describing words of your own that tell about Rosie. Draw an outline of a dog, and use the words you collected to write a shape poem about Rosie the visiting dog.

ACTIVITIES

Dog Stories

MAKE A READING LIST

Rosie is a real-life dog hero who helps people feel better. Many books have been written about dogs and dog heroes. Use the card catalog or a computer catalog in a library to find dog books for readers your age. Make a list of these books, and share your list with your classmates.

Word Picture

WRITE A DESCRIPTION

Think of a dog or another pet that you know and like. Write a paragraph that will help your readers form a picture of the pet in their minds. Tell how the pet looks, feels, and sounds. Explain what you like about the pet, and what makes it special to you.

Main Idea

Rosie is a special dog who visits people and makes them happy. That is the **main idea** of the selection, or the message the author wants to tell. To find the main idea, ask yourself, "What is this selection mostly about?"

Sometimes the main idea is **stated,** or told right in the story or paragraph. Look at the paragraph and the web below. The main idea is in the center circle of the web. The other sentences tell more about the main idea. Find the main idea in the paragraph.

Before she could be a visiting dog, Rosie had to learn many things. She learned to play games. She learned to get along with other dogs. She learned to be comfortable with all kinds of people.

She learned to play games.

She learned to be comfortable with all kinds of people.

Before she could be a visiting dog, Rosie had to learn many things.

She learned to get along with other dogs.

Finding the main idea can help you understand what you read. Read the paragraph below. What is the main idea? Tell it in your own words.

Rosie visited many people at the nursing home. Some people there wanted to cuddle Rosie. Some people liked to talk to her. One man remembered his own dog. All of the people who met Rosie wanted her to visit again.

WHAT HAVE YOU LEARNED?

1. What question can you ask to find the main idea of a story or a paragraph?

2. On page 293, Rosie is taught a command so that she will not be rude. What is the main idea of that paragraph? Tell the main idea in your own words.

Visit **The Learning Site!**
www.harcourtschool.com

TRY THIS • TRY THIS • TRY THIS

With a partner, take turns reading a short magazine article. Each person should write a sentence that tells the main idea of the article. Read your sentences aloud to each other. Did you and your partner tell the main idea in exactly the same words? Do your sentences mean the same thing?

307

CENTERFIELD BALLHAWK

by Matt Christopher
illustrated by Larry Johnson

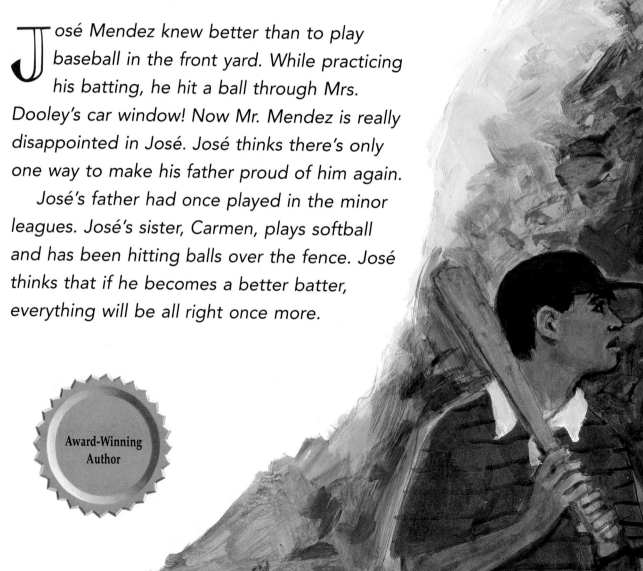

José Mendez knew better than to play baseball in the front yard. While practicing his batting, he hit a ball through Mrs. Dooley's car window! Now Mr. Mendez is really disappointed in José. José thinks there's only one way to make his father proud of him again.

José's father had once played in the minor leagues. José's sister, Carmen, plays softball and has been hitting balls over the fence. José thinks that if he becomes a better batter, everything will be all right once more.

Award-Winning
Author

"Steeerike!" yelled the ump. Then, "Steeerike two!"

"Belt it, José!" cried the coach.

José's heart pounded like crazy. This was it.

Crack! His bat met the ball head-on. The white sphere took off like a rocket for left field and sailed over the fence for a home run!

The Mudders' fans screamed their heads off. "All right, José!" they shouted as he dropped his bat and trotted around the bases.

Bus singled that inning, too, but the Mudders failed to score him. Mudders 5, Bulls 2.

The Stockade Bulls came to bat blowing through their nostrils. After two outs and a man on third base, Adzie Healy lambasted one. It had a home run label on it as it zoomed toward the center field fence. José started to run back the instant he had seen it hit.

He was almost up against the fence when the ball came flying down over his head. He jumped—and caught it!

"Yes! Great catch, man!" Barry yelled. "Saved us a run!"

José smiled and tossed the ball to him as they ran in together. "Just lucky," he said.

"Sure." Barry laughed.

Alfie singled, and Turtleneck walked, bringing José up to the plate. *I've got to get a hit*, he thought. *I've got to, or I'm sunk.*

He grounded out.

Good thing Dad isn't at the game, he thought as he returned to the bench. At least he's got Carmen.

The Mudders kept the Bulls from scoring in the bottom of the fourth and then went to town at their turn at bat, scoring two runs. Mudders 7, Bulls 2.

In the bottom of the fifth, the Stockade Bulls showed the real power they had, as if they had purposely kept it hidden until now. They pounded Sparrow for five runs, tying up the score, 7 to 7.

In the top of the sixth, Barry singled, then Turtleneck flied out. José slowly stepped to the plate. This could be it, he thought. A hit now could break the tie. And it would mean a .500 average for him.

He flied out.

José's heart sank into his stomach. He wished he could vanish.

Then T.V. struck out, and the Bulls were back up to the plate.

The first two guys got on. Then Ted Jackson popped up to the pitcher, and Adzie blasted a line drive to center field. It looked as if it were going to hit the ground halfway between second base and José.

José was after it like a gazelle. He knew he had to catch that ball or the game was over.

He dove, then felt the solid *thud!* as the ball landed squarely in his glove.

The crowd stood up, and clapped and cheered for a full minute.

On the next play, a grounder skittered through T.V.'s legs. A run scored, and the game was over. The Stockade Bulls beat the Peach Street Mudders, 8 to 7.

"It's my fault we lost! My fault!" T.V. moaned as José caught up with him and they walked off the field together.

"Don't sweat it, man!" José said. "It's not the end of the world! Who's perfect?"

He was thinking of his batting as he said it. One out of four was .250. Far, far from a .375 average. His father would never, *never* think much of him as a baseball player.

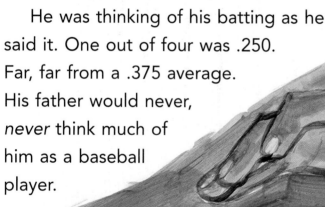

Suddenly he heard his name called. "José! Wait up!"

He turned.

"Dad!" he cried, surprised. "When did you get here?"

"At the beginning of the fourth inning," Mr. Mendez said.

José's face clouded. "Then you saw . . ." he started to say, but couldn't go on. How could he face his father when he'd gotten out three out of four times at bat?

"What do you want to say, son?" Mr. Mendez asked, putting his arm across José's shoulders.

"I wanted to make you proud of me," José blurted out. "I know I've been messing up lately, but I thought if I could hit .375, like you did when you played in the minors, I could make up for disappointing you. I—I'm sorry, Dad. I know I've let you down."

Mr. Mendez stopped short and looked down at José. "Is that why you've been so down in the mouth?" he exclaimed.

José sighed, then nodded.

"Listen, son," Mr. Mendez said, "I may be disappointed when you go against my wishes—like you did when you hit Mrs. Dooley's car—but I'm not disappointed in *you*. I trust you when you say you're sorry, and that's that. As far as Mrs. Dooley is concerned, I know you've worked hard to make it up to her. From what I hear," he added, smiling, "you even applied a little extra elbow grease to her car the other day."

José blushed.

Then Mr. Mendez took a deep breath and went on: "It's been hard since Mom died . . . on all of us. I've had to depend on you and Carmen to pull your own weight . . . maybe too much." He grinned. "I seem to have forgotten how hard it can be to concentrate on anything when it's baseball season. Maybe we both need to be more aware of what the other person is feeling. I'll try, if you will."

José nodded happily.

"And one more thing. Forget about trying to hit like I did, okay? You don't have to. You're a born outfielder, José! You've made catches that I never would have been able to, not in a million years."

José stared at him. "Really? You mean you . . . don't mind that I can't hit?"

José's father chuckled. "'Can't hit?' If you call belting a grand slam homer not hitting, well, son, we've got to sit down and have a serious talk about the game of baseball! José, you're a born ballhawk, so stop worrying about the hitting and concentrate on your fielding. That's where your team needs you the most."

José couldn't believe his ears. All this time he had thought . . . But then he recalled the joyous cheers after each catch he had made that day and smiled.

"Thanks, Dad," he murmured. "I never thought about that. I just figured the guys were being nice when they said they counted on me being in the outfield." He glanced up at his father. "I like having people depend on me, Dad."

His father squeezed his shoulder. "Come on. We'll pick up some ice cream and celebrate those catches with Carmen. I understand she's had a hard afternoon, smashing one homer after another for her team. Looks like both of you kids are a chip off the old block, eh?"

José laughed. He never felt better in his life as he walked with his father to the car.

I might never get a .375 average, he thought. But I'm a hit with my father, and that's what counts the most.

THINK ABOUT IT

1 Why does José think he needs to be a great batter?

2 What does José learn about himself and his father?

3 What did you like best about this story?

About the Author

MATT CHRISTOPHER

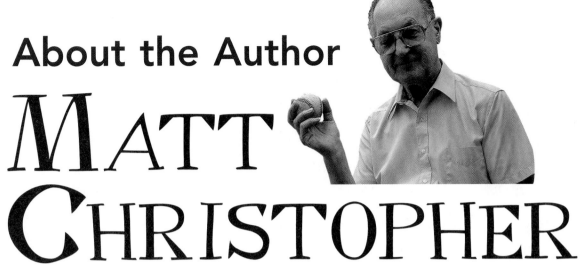

As a boy, Matt Christopher had two favorite things: sports and writing. He played all kinds of sports, but his favorite was baseball. When he first started playing baseball, he sometimes got discouraged because he wasn't a star hitter. When he got older, he played so well that he earned a Most Valuable Player award.

Later, instead of playing sports, Matt Christopher began writing about them. During his life, he wrote more than seventy-five books. "I love writing, and do as most writers do: work on an idea until it's the best I can come up with. Then . . . work on another . . . and another . . . and so on!" he once said.

Visit *The Learning Site!*
www.harcourtschool.com

SPOTLIGHT ON BASEBALL

Baseball is a popular game in many parts of the world. The diagram below shows how a baseball field is set up. The text on page 327 gives more information about the centerfielder.

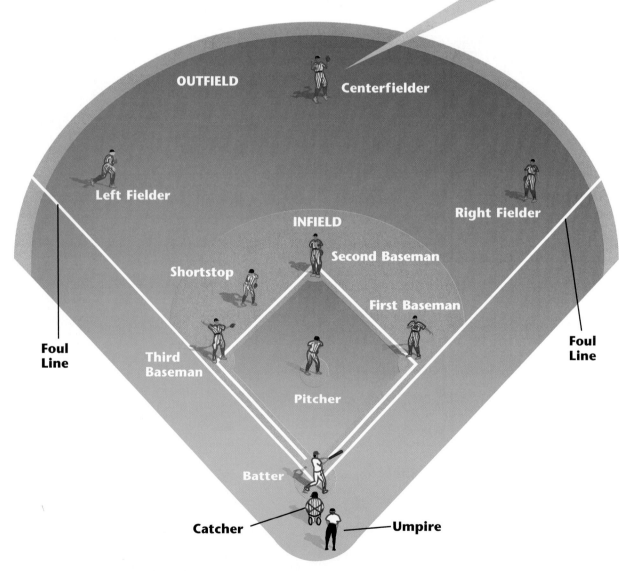

OUTFIELD

Centerfielder

Left Fielder

Right Fielder

INFIELD

Shortstop

Second Baseman

First Baseman

Foul
Line

Foul
Line

Third
Baseman

Pitcher

Batter

Catcher

Umpire

José Mendez plays center field for his baseball team, the Peach Street Mudders. Center field is one of the most important positions in baseball. Read below to find out more about what a centerfielder does.

Centerfielder

The centerfielder should be the best all-around outfielder on the team. The centerfielder is considered the captain of the outfield. He or she should be the outfielder with the most speed. This is because the centerfielder has the most ground to cover. The centerfielder must also have a very strong arm. He or she has to make long throws and move like a cat. The centerfielder must be able to quickly run in, run back, or run to either side.

The centerfielder should try to catch any fly balls he or she can reach. The other outfielders run for fly balls until they hear the centerfielder "call them off."

Center field is fun. It is also a very important position. Some of the best players in history have played center field.

THINK ABOUT IT

Why is center field an important position in baseball?

327

RESPONSE ACTIVITIES

Want to Trade?

DESIGN A TRADING CARD

Major-league ballplayers have their pictures
on trading cards. Design your own trading card. Paste a
photograph or a drawing of yourself on the front. On the
back, write things people would want to know about you.
Trade cards with a classmate.

Rules of the Game

RESEARCH A SPORT

Every sport has its own rules
of play. Choose a sport, and use
an encyclopedia in the library
or on CD-ROM to research
the rules of the game. Write a
short report that tells about
the rules. Share your
report with
classmates.

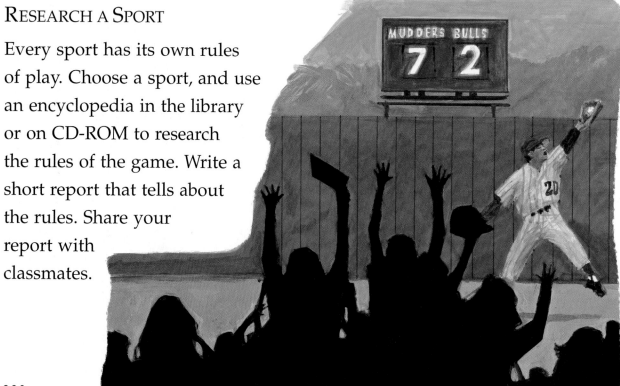

Making Connections

CREATE A BASEBALL GLOSSARY

The author of "Centerfield Ballhawk"
uses many baseball terms, such as
singled, flied out, and *grand slam homer.*
List these terms and others you
learned from "Spotlight on Baseball."
Write a definition for each term.
Then rewrite the terms and their
definitions in alphabetical order
to create a baseball glossary.

Let's Chat

ROLE-PLAY

José was worried about playing
well in the baseball game.
After the game was over
and he talked with his
father, he felt better. Imagine
that José called a friend
to talk about what he
learned. With a
classmate, role-play the
conversation they
might have had.

Ramona Forever

by Beverly Cleary

illustrated by Diane Greenseid

After Uncle Hobart's exciting wedding, the Quimby family is about to have another big event— the birth of the fifth Quimby. The baby, whom they have all nicknamed Algie, is due to be born any minute.

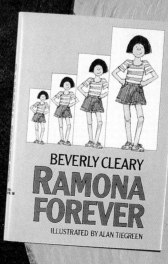

BEVERLY CLEARY
RAMONA FOREVER
ILLUSTRATED BY ALAN TIEGREEN

Mrs. Quimby pushed her chair farther from the table and glanced at her watch. All eyes were on her.

"Shall I call the doctor?" asked Mr. Quimby.

"Please," said Mrs. Quimby as she rose from the table, hugged Algie, and breathed, "Oo-oo."

Ramona and Beezus, excited and frightened, looked at one another. At last! The fifth Quimby would soon be here. Nothing would be the same again, ever. Mr. Quimby reported that the doctor would meet them at the hospital. Without being asked, Beezus ran for the bag her mother had packed several weeks ago.

Mrs. Quimby kissed her daughters. "Don't look so frightened," she said. "Everything is going to be all right. Be good girls, and Daddy will be home as soon as he can." She bent forward and hugged Algie again.

The house suddenly seemed empty. The girls listened to the car back out of the driveway. The sound of the motor became lost in traffic.

"Well," said Beezus, "I suppose we might as well do the dishes."

"I suppose so." Ramona tested all the doors, including the door to the basement, to make sure they were locked.

"Too bad Picky-picky isn't here to eat all this tuna salad no one felt like eating." Beezus scraped the plates into the garbage.

To her own surprise, Ramona burst into tears and buried her face in a dish towel. "I just want Mother to come home," she wept.

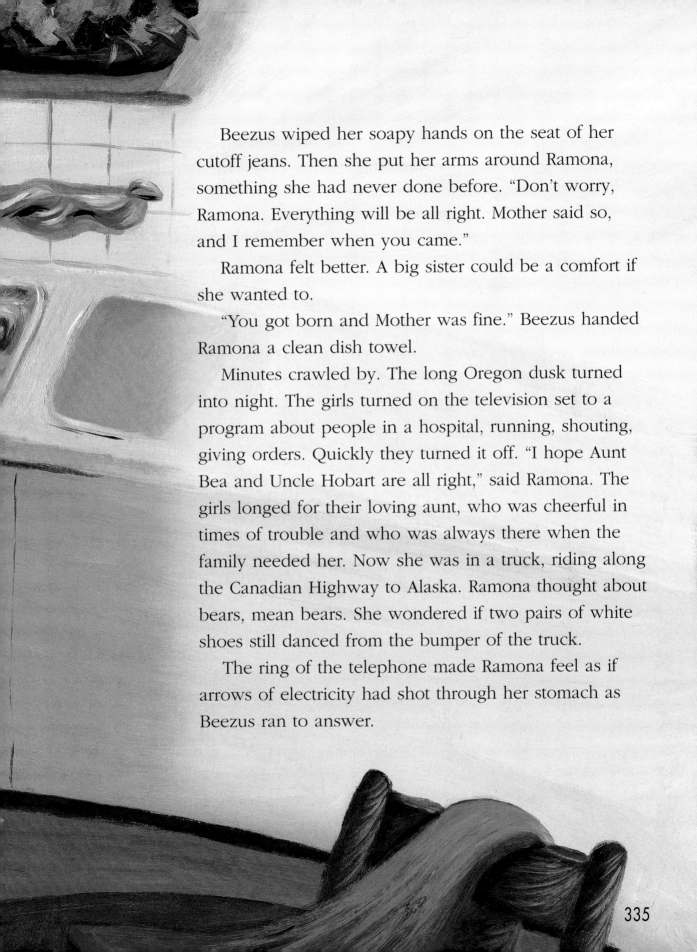

Beezus wiped her soapy hands on the seat of her cutoff jeans. Then she put her arms around Ramona, something she had never done before. "Don't worry, Ramona. Everything will be all right. Mother said so, and I remember when you came."

Ramona felt better. A big sister could be a comfort if she wanted to.

"You got born and Mother was fine." Beezus handed Ramona a clean dish towel.

Minutes crawled by. The long Oregon dusk turned into night. The girls turned on the television set to a program about people in a hospital, running, shouting, giving orders. Quickly they turned it off. "I hope Aunt Bea and Uncle Hobart are all right," said Ramona. The girls longed for their loving aunt, who was cheerful in times of trouble and who was always there when the family needed her. Now she was in a truck, riding along the Canadian Highway to Alaska. Ramona thought about bears, mean bears. She wondered if two pairs of white shoes still danced from the bumper of the truck.

The ring of the telephone made Ramona feel as if arrows of electricity had shot through her stomach as Beezus ran to answer.

"Oh." There was disappointment in Beezus's voice. "All right, Daddy. No. No, we don't mind." When the conversation ended, she turned to Ramona, who was wild for news, and said, "Algie is taking his time. Daddy wants to stay with Mom and wanted to be sure we didn't mind staying alone. I said we didn't, and he said we were brave girls."

"Oh," said Ramona, who longed for her father's return. "Well, I'm brave, I guess." Even though the evening was unusually warm, she closed all the windows.

"I suppose we should go to bed," said Beezus. "If you want, you can get in bed with me."

"We better leave lights on for Daddy." Ramona turned on the porch light, as well as all the lights in the living room and hall, before she climbed into her sister's bed. "So Daddy won't fall over anything," she explained.

"Good idea," agreed Beezus. Each sister knew the other felt safer with the lights on.

"I hope Algie will hurry," said Ramona.

"So do I," agreed Beezus.

The girls slept lightly until the sound of a key in the door awoke them. "Daddy?" Beezus called out.

"Yes." Mr. Quimby came down the hall to the door of Beezus's room. "Great news. Roberta Day Quimby, six pounds, four ounces, arrived safe and sound. Your mother is fine."

Barely awake, Ramona asked, "Who's Roberta?"

"Your new sister," answered her father, "and my namesake."

"Sister." Now Ramona was wide-awake. The family had referred to the baby as Algie so long she had assumed that of course she would have a brother.

"Yes, a beautiful little sister," said her father. "Now, go back to sleep. It's four o'clock in the morning, and I've got to get up at seven-thirty."

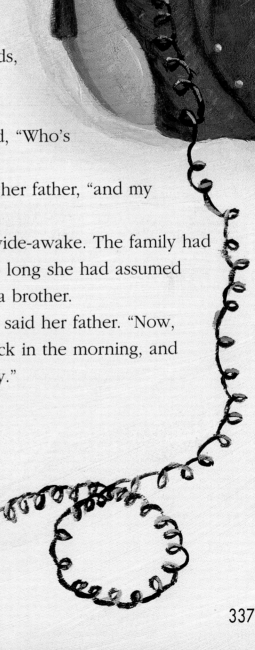

The next morning, Mr. Quimby overslept and ate his breakfast standing up. He was halfway out the door when he called back, "When I get off work, we'll have dinner at the Whopperburger, and then we'll all go see Roberta and your mother."

The day was long and lonely. Even a swimming lesson at the park and a trip to the library did little to make time pass. "I wonder what Roberta looks like?" said Beezus.

"And whose room she will share when she outgrows the bassinette?" worried Ramona.

The one happy moment in the day for the girls was a telephone call from their mother, who reported that Roberta was a beautiful, healthy little sister. She couldn't wait to bring her home, and she was proud of her daughters for being so good about staying alone. This pleased Beezus and Ramona so much they ran the vacuum cleaner and dusted, which made time pass faster until their father, looking exhausted, came home to take them out for hamburgers and a visit to the fifth Quimby.

Ramona could feel her heart pounding as she finally climbed the steps to the hospital. Visitors, some carrying flowers and others looking careworn, walked toward the elevators. Nurses hurried, a doctor was paged over the loudspeaker. Ramona could scarcely bear her own excitement. The rising of the elevator made her stomach feel as if it had stayed behind on the first floor. When the elevator stopped, Mr. Quimby led the way down the hall.

"Excuse me," called a nurse.

Surprised, the family stopped and turned.

"Children under twelve are not allowed to visit the maternity ward," said the nurse. "Little girl, you will have to go down and wait in the lobby."

"Why is that?" asked Mr. Quimby.

"Children under twelve might have contagious diseases," explained the nurse. "We have to protect the babies."

"I'm sorry, Ramona," said Mr. Quimby. "I didn't know. I am afraid you will have to do as the nurse says."

"Does she mean I'm *germy*?" Ramona was humiliated. "I took a shower this morning and washed my hands at the Whopperburger so I would be extra clean."

"Sometimes children are coming down with something and don't know it," explained Mr. Quimby. "Now, be a big girl and go downstairs and wait for us."

Ramona's eyes filled with tears of disappointment, but she found some pleasure in riding in the elevator alone. By the time she reached the lobby, she felt worse. The nurse called her a little girl. Her father called her a big girl. What was she? A germy girl.

Ramona sat gingerly on the edge of a Naugahyde couch. If she leaned back, she might get germs on it, or it might get germs on her. She swallowed hard. Was her throat a little bit sore? She thought maybe it was, way down in back. She put her hand to her forehead the way her mother did when she thought Ramona might have a fever. Her forehead was warm, maybe too warm.

As Ramona waited, she began to itch the way she itched when she had chickenpox. Her head itched, her back itched, her legs itched. Ramona scratched. A woman sat down on the couch, looked at Ramona, got up, and moved to another couch.

Ramona felt worse. She itched more and scratched harder. She swallowed often to see how her sore throat was coming along. She peeked down the neck of her blouse to see if she might have a rash and was surprised that she did not. She sniffed from time to time to see if she had a runny nose.

Now Ramona was angry. It would serve everybody right if she came down with some horrible disease, right there in their old hospital. That would show everybody how germfree the place was. Ramona squirmed and gave that hard-to-reach place between her shoulder blades a good hard scratch. Then she scratched her head with both hands. People stopped to stare.

A man in a white coat, with a stethoscope hanging out of his pocket, came hurrying through the lobby, glanced at Ramona, stopped, and took a good look at her. "How do you feel?" he asked.

"Awful," she admitted. "A nurse said I was too germy to go see my mother and new sister, but I think I caught some disease right here."

"I see," said the doctor. "Open your mouth and say 'ah.'"

Ramona *ahhed* until she gagged.

"Mh-hm," murmured the doctor. He looked so serious Ramona was alarmed. Then he pulled out his stethoscope and listened to her front and back, thumping as he did so. What was he hearing? Was there something wrong with her insides? Why didn't her father come?

The doctor nodded as if his worst suspicions had been confirmed. "Just as I thought," he said, pulling out his prescription pad.

Medicine, ugh. Ramona's twitching stopped. Her nose and throat felt fine. "I feel much better," she assured the doctor as she eyed that prescription pad with distrust.

"An acute case of siblingitis. Not at all unusual around here, but it shouldn't last long." He tore off the prescription he had written, instructed Ramona to give it to her father, and hurried on down the hall.

Ramona could not remember the name of her illness. She tried to read the doctor's scribbly cursive writing, but she could not. She could only read neat cursive, the sort her teacher wrote on the blackboard.

Itching again, she was still staring at the slip of paper when Mr. Quimby and Beezus stepped out of the elevator. "Roberta is so tiny." Beezus was radiant with joy. "And she is perfectly darling. She has a little round nose and—oh, when you see her, you'll love her."

"I'm sick." Ramona tried to sound pitiful. "I've got something awful. A doctor said so."

Beezus paid no attention. "And Roberta has brown hair—"

Mr. Quimby interrupted. "What's this all about, Ramona?"

"A doctor said I had something, some kind of *itis*, and I have to have this right away." She handed her father her prescription and scratched one shoulder. "If I don't, I might get sicker."

Mr. Quimby read the scribbly cursive, and then he did a strange thing. He lifted Ramona and gave her a big hug and a kiss, right there in the lobby. The itching stopped. Ramona felt much better. "You have acute siblingitis," explained her father. "*Itis* means inflammation."

Ramona already knew the meaning of sibling. Since her father had studied to be a teacher, brothers and sisters had become siblings to him.

"He understood you were worried and angry because you weren't allowed to see your new sibling, and prescribed attention," explained Mr. Quimby. "Now let's all go buy ice-cream cones before I fall asleep standing up."

Beezus said Roberta was too darling to be called a dumb word like sibling. Ramona felt silly, but she also felt better.

For the next three nights, Ramona took a book to the hospital and sat in the lobby, not reading, but sulking about the injustice of having to wait to see the strange new Roberta.

On the fourth day, Mr. Quimby took an hour off from the Shop-rite Market, picked up Beezus and Ramona, who were waiting in clean clothes, and drove to the hospital to bring home his wife and new daughter.

Ramona moved closer to Beezus when she saw her mother, holding a pink bundle, emerge from the elevator in a wheelchair pushed by a nurse and followed by Mr. Quimby carrying her bag. "Can't Mother walk?" she whispered.

"Of course she can walk," answered Beezus. "The hospital wants to make sure people get out without falling down and suing for a million dollars."

Mrs. Quimby waved to the girls. Roberta's face was hidden by a corner of a pink blanket, but the nurse had no time for a little girl eager to see a new baby. She pushed the wheelchair through the automatic door to the waiting car.

"*Now* can I see her?" begged Ramona when her mother and Roberta were settled in the front, and the girls had climbed into the backseat.

"Dear Heart, of course you may." Mrs. Quimby then spoke the most beautiful words Ramona had ever heard, "Oh, Ramona, how I've missed you," as she turned back the blanket.

Ramona, leaning over the front seat for her first

glimpse of the new baby sister, tried to hold her breath so she wouldn't breathe germs on Roberta, who did not look at all like the picture on the cover of *A Name for Your Baby*. Her face was bright pink, almost red, and her hair, unlike the smooth pale hair of the baby on the cover of the pamphlet, was dark and wild. Ramona did not know what to say. She did not feel that words like darling or adorable fitted this baby.

"She looks exactly like you looked when you were born," Mrs. Quimby told Ramona.

"She does?" Ramona found this hard to believe. She could not imagine that she had once looked like this red, frowning little creature.

"Well, what do you think of your new sister?" asked Mr. Quimby.

"She's so — so *little*," Ramona answered truthfully.

Roberta opened her blue gray eyes.

"Mother!" cried Ramona. "She's cross-eyed."

Mrs. Quimby laughed. "All babies look cross-eyed sometimes. They outgrow it when they learn to focus." Sure enough, Roberta's eyes straightened out for a moment and then crossed again. She worked her mouth as if she didn't know what to do with it. She made little snuffling noises and lifted one arm as if she didn't know what it was for.

"Why does her nightie have those little pockets at the ends of the sleeves?" asked Ramona. "They cover up her hands."

"They keep her from scratching herself," explained Mrs. Quimby. "She's too little to understand that fingernails scratch."

Ramona sat back and buckled her seat belt. She had once looked like Roberta. Amazing! She had once been that tiny, but she had grown, her hair had calmed down when she remembered to comb it, and she had learned to use her eyes and hands. "You know what I think?" she asked and did not wait for an answer. "I think it is hard work to be a baby." Ramona spoke as if she had discovered something unknown to the rest of the world. With her words came unexpected love and sympathy for the tiny person in her mother's arms.

"I hadn't thought of it that way," said Mrs. Quimby, "but I think you're right."

"Growing up is hard work," said Mr. Quimby as he drove away from the hospital. "Sometimes being grown-up is hard work."

"I know," said Ramona and thought some more. She thought about loose teeth, real sore throats, quarrels, misunderstandings with her teachers, longing for a bicycle her family could not afford, worrying when her parents bickered, how terrible she had felt when she hurt Beezus's feelings without meaning to, and all the long afternoons when Mrs. Kemp looked after her until her mother came from work. She had survived it all. "Isn't it funny?" she remarked as her father steered the car into their driveway.

"Isn't what funny?" asked her mother.

"That I used to be little and funny-looking and cross-eyed like Roberta," said Ramona. "And now look at me. I'm wonderful me!"

"Except when you're blunderful you," said Beezus.

Ramona did not mind when her family, except Roberta, who was too little, laughed. "Yup, wonderful, blunderful me," she said and was happy. She was winning at growing up.

Think About It

1 Why does Ramona think she is "winning at growing up"?

2 If you saw Ramona the day after her mother came home, what would you ask her? What do you think she might say?

3 What is Ramona's problem? How do her parents help her?

Meet the Author
Beverly Cleary

How does Beverly Cleary write? Read this interview to find out.

Question: How do you actually do your writing?
Beverly Cleary: Oh, I write with a pen first. Then I type up what I've written so I can see what it looks like.

Question: What is the hardest thing for you about writing, and what is the easiest thing?
Beverly Cleary: The hardest thing about writing is pushing through to the end of the story. The easiest thing is revising. I think all writers do some revising. That is when I cross out a lot and shorten a page to one paragraph.

Question: When you start a book, do you know how it's going to end?
Beverly Cleary: I often begin in the middle. I begin with the characters and something they would do and just let the story work itself out.

ALL MY HATS

by Richard J. Margolis
illustrated by Robert Casilla

All my hats
are hats he wore.
What a bore.

All my pants
are pants he ripped.
What a gyp.

All my books
are books he read.
What a head.

All my fights
are fights he fought.
What a thought.

All my steps
are steps he tried.
What a guide.

All my teachers
call me by my brother's name.
What a shame.

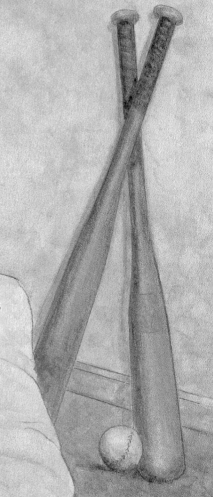

Response Activities

A Case of Siblingitis

PANTOMIME A SCENE

With some classmates, act out the scene in which a nurse tells Ramona to wait in the lobby and a doctor tells her she has siblingitis. Before you start, think about how Ramona acts when she thinks she is sick. Then act out the scene using only movements. Try not to use any words at all.

Big Brother, Big Sister

WRITE A PARAGRAPH

Ramona is not the baby of the family anymore. How do you think she will like being a big sister? Write a paragraph describing the good things about being an older brother or sister.

Blunderful Me!

MAKE A LIST

Wonderful, blunderful Ramona! Growing up
is hard work, but Ramona is doing quite
well. Make a list of several things you have
learned since you started school. Explain to
a friend how you have grown up.

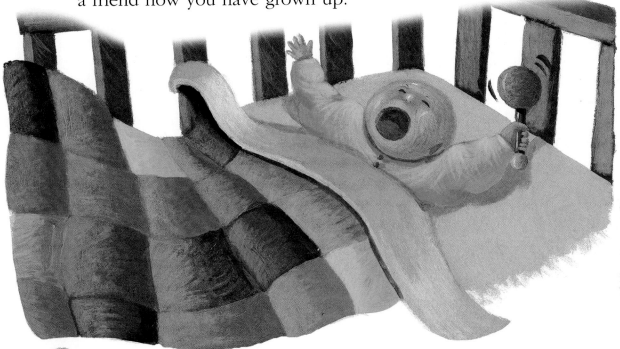

Making Connections

WRITE LETTERS

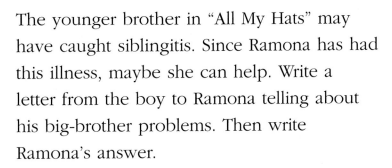

The younger brother in "All My Hats" may
have caught siblingitis. Since Ramona has had
this illness, maybe she can help. Write a
letter from the boy to Ramona telling about
his big-brother problems. Then write
Ramona's answer.

Theme Wrap-Up

Character Picture Album

DRAW A CHARACTER Often, the main character in a story changes in some way because of another character. Julian, for example, changes his mind about having a girl for a friend. Choose three stories from this theme. For each story, draw a picture of the friend or family member who causes the main character to change, and tell why you chose this character to illustrate.

Introduce New Friends

WRITE A LETTER Choose one character from this theme, and write a letter to him or her. In your letter, tell about a character from another story in the theme. Explain why you think the two characters might become friends if they met.

Talk Radio

ROLE-PLAY A RADIO SHOW With a small group, role-play a radio talk show. One group member can play the host. The others can play characters from the stories in this theme. Work together to write questions the host can ask the characters. Practice your role-play, and then perform the radio show for classmates.

Using the Glossary

Like a dictionary, this glossary lists words in alphabetical order. To find a word, look it up by its first letter or letters.

To save time, use the **guide words** at the top of each page. These show you the first and last words on the page. Look at the guide words to see if your word falls between them alphabetically.

Here is an example of a glossary entry:

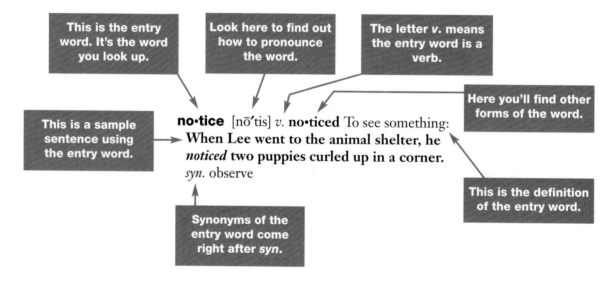

This is the entry word. It's the word you look up.

Look here to find out how to pronounce the word.

The letter *v.* means the entry word is a verb.

Here you'll find other forms of the word.

This is a sample sentence using the entry word.

no·tice [nō′tis] *v.* **no·ticed** To see something: **When Lee went to the animal shelter, he** *noticed* **two puppies curled up in a corner.** *syn.* observe

This is the definition of the entry word.

Synonyms of the entry word come right after *syn.*

Word Origins

Throughout the glossary, you will find notes about word origins, or how words get started and change. Words often have interesting backgrounds that can help you remember what they mean.

Here is an example of a word origin note:

familiar At first, *familiar* meant "of the family," from the Latin word *familiaris*. Its meaning grew to include friends and to become "known from being around often." *Familiar* began to be used in English in the 1300s.

Pronunciation

The pronunciation in brackets is a respelling that shows how the word is pronounced.

The **pronunciation key** explains what the symbols in a respelling mean. A shortened pronunciation key appears on every other page of the glossary.

PRONUNCIATION KEY*

a	add, map	m	move, seem	u	up, done
ā	ace, rate	n	nice, tin	û(r)	burn, term
â(r)	care, air	ng	ring, song	yōo	fuse, few
ä	palm, father	o	odd, hot	v	vain, eve
b	bat, rub	ō	open, so	w	win, away
ch	check, catch	ô	order, jaw	y	yet, yearn
d	dog, rod	oi	oil, boy	z	zest, muse
e	end, pet	ou	pout, now	zh	vision, pleasure
ē	equal, tree	ŏŏ	took, full	ə	the schwa, an
f	fit, half	ōō	pool, food		unstressed vowel
g	go, log	p	pit, stop		representing the
h	hope, hate	r	run, poor		sound spelled
i	it, give	s	see, pass		*a* in *above*
ī	ice, write	sh	sure, rush		*e* in *sicken*
j	joy, ledge	t	talk, sit		*i* in *possible*
k	cool, take	th	thin, both		*o* in *melon*
l	look, rule	t̶h̶	this, bathe		*u* in *circus*

Other symbols
- separates words into syllables
- ´ indicates heavier stress on a syllable
- ´ indicates light stress on a syllable

Abbreviations: *adj.* adjective, *adv.* adverb, *conj.* conjunction, *interj.* interjection, *n.* noun, *prep.* preposition, *pron.* pronoun, *syn.* synonym, *v.* verb

* The Pronunciation Key, adapted entries, and the Short Key that appear on the following pages are reprinted from *HBJ School Dictionary* Copyright © 1990 by Harcourt Brace & Company. Reprinted by permission of Harcourt Brace & Company.

ac·ci·dent [ak′sə·dənt] *n.* An event that happens without warning, sometimes causing harm or damage: **Pedro broke his arm in an *accident*.**

aim [ām] *v.* **aimed** To point an object at a target: **Carol *aimed* the soccer ball at the goal.**

aim

ap·plaud [ə·plôd′] *v.* **ap·plaud·ed** To clap hands to show excitement or happiness: **When Julie finished singing, we *applauded* loudly.**

ap·point·ment [ə·point′mənt] *n.* A time to be somewhere or to meet someone: **Laronda was on time for her *appointment* with the dentist.**

ap·proach [ə·prōch′] *v.* To come closer to; to move toward: **As you *approach* the music room, you will hear the band playing.**

at·ten·tion [ə·ten′shən] *n.* The act of noticing, listening to, or thinking about someone or something: **Pay *attention* to cars, bicycles, and traffic signals when you cross the street.**

at·tract [ə·trakt′] *v.* To pull or draw objects together: **This magnet will *attract* and hold steel nails.**

au·di·ence [ô′dē·əns] *n.* A group of people watching and listening to a performance: **The *audience* clapped until Aretha sang another song.**

Word Origins

audience The word *audience* comes from the Latin word *audire*, meaning "to hear." An audience hears when something is read or spoken out loud. It came into the English language in the 1300s.

ball·hawk [bôl′hôk] *n.* A nickname given to a ballplayer who is good at catching balls, especially ones that are hard to catch: **When Joey made another amazing catch, his teammates began to call him a *ballhawk*.**

be·yond [bē·yond′] *prep.* Outside of; farther away than: **Dad told me not to ride my bike *beyond* the corner of our street.**

bil·lion [bil′yən] *n.* **bil·lions** A thousand million; an amount that seems too great to count or know: **There are *billions* of grains of sand on the beach.**

brunch [brunch] *n.* A meal that combines breakfast and lunch: **That restaurant serves *brunch* from 11:00 A.M. until 2:00 P.M. every Sunday.**

busi·ness [biz′nis] *n.* The offering of a service or a product to customers in return for payment: **Jake started a lawn-mowing *business* and earned enough money to buy a new bike.**

cart·wheel [kärt′(h)wēl′] *n.* A sideways movement in which the body turns like a wheel: **You need good balance to turn a *cartwheel* without falling over.**

cartwheel

cham·pi·on·ships [cham′pē·ən·ships′] *n.* A series of games played to decide which player or team is the best: **The girls' soccer team won a trophy at the state *championships*.**

cheer [chir] *v.* **cheered** To shout to encourage or praise someone: **When Bobby scored the winning goal, everyone *cheered*.**

> **Word Origins**
> **cheer** At first, *cheer* meant "face," taken from the Latin word *cara*, meaning "face." The way a person feels often shows on his or her face. At the start of the 1700s, *cheer* came to mean "to shout praise or encouragement."

col·lapse [kə·laps′] *v.* **col·lapsed** To fall down from being very tired, hot, or sick: **After running the last part of the race at full speed, Sara *collapsed* just as she won.**

com·fort [kum′fərt] *n.* Someone or something that makes others feel better when they are in pain or unhappy: **Terry played with the younger children and was a *comfort* to them while their mother was away.**

com·fort·a·ble [kum′fər·tə·bəl] *adj.* At ease: **Roland felt *comfortable* in his aunt's house.** *syn.* content

com·mand [kə·mand′] *n.* **com·mands** An order to do something: **When the captain shouted *commands*, the soldiers quickly did what they were told.**

com·plain [kəm·plān′] *v.* **com·plained** To find fault; to tell someone in charge about something that seems to be wrong: **Teresa *complained* to the landlord about the leaky faucet.**

con·cen·trate [kon′sən·trāt′] *v.* To give complete attention to; to think hard about: **It was hard to *concentrate* on the test because of the noise from the playground.**

con·fi·dent [kon′fə·dənt] *adj.* Sure of something: **Ramon was *confident* that he had done well on the math test.** *syn.* certain

con·nect [kə·nekt′] *v.* **con·nect·ed** To attach; to join together: **The two sides of the river will be *connected* by a bridge.**

a	add	e	end	o	odd	o͞o	pool	oi	oil	t͟h	this
ā	ace	ē	equal	ō	open	u	up	ou	pout	zh	vision
â	care	i	it	ô	order	û	burn	ng	ring		
ä	palm	ī	ice	o͝o	took	yo͞o	fuse	th	thin		

ə = {
a in *above*
e in *sicken*
i in *possible*
o in *melon*
u in *circus*
}

con·ta·gious [kən•tā′jəs] *adj.* Spread easily from one person to another; usually used to describe a disease: **Many people get the flu because it is very *contagious*.**

coun·sel·or [koun′səl•ər *or* koun′slər] *n.* A person who watches over children in camp, guiding them and helping them learn skills: **Our *counselor* showed us how to mark a trail through the woods.**

cre·a·tive [krē•ā′tiv] *adj.* Showing imagination in thinking, writing, or making things: **You could see that the children were *creative* from their interesting paintings and stories.**

crea·ture [krē′chər] *n.* **crea·tures** Any living being; an animal or person: **Some people think spiders are scary *creatures*.**

creatures

cu·ri·ous [kyōōr′ē•əs] *adj.* Full of questions about things and wanting to know the answers: **If you're so *curious* about what's inside the box, open it and find out.** *syn.* interested

dec·o·rate [dek′ə•rāt] *v.* **dec·o·rat·ed** To make something prettier by adding to it: **Family pictures *decorated* the living room walls.**

Word Origins

decorate *Decorate* comes from the Latin *decoratus*, meaning "made beautiful." That word comes from the Latin word for ornament, *decus*.

del·i·cate [del′ə•kit] *adj.* Describes something that needs to be treated with care because it is breakable: **The *delicate* hand-painted eggs were placed in special holders.** *syns.* weak; fragile

de·part·ment [di•pärt′mənt] *n.* A part or section of a government or a company with members who have special duties: **A man from the fire *department* spoke to the students about fire safety.**

de·pend [di•pend′] *v.* To trust or count on someone to do something: **You can *depend* on us to clean up after the party.**

drift [drift] *n.* **drifts** A large pile of something, such as snow, that is formed by the wind: **During the blizzard, the wind blew the snow into *drifts* as high as twelve feet.**

ea·ger [ē′gər] *adj.* Full of excited interest: **Zoey was so *eager* to see the newborn kittens that she ran all the way home.**

en·joy [in·joi′] *v.* **en·joy·ing** To get happiness or delight from: **You can tell by their happy faces that the girls are *enjoying* the party.**

e·quip·ment [i·kwip′mənt] *n.* Things used for a special purpose: **The new store sells skates, balls, helmets, and other sports *equipment*. *syn.* supplies**

e·rupt [i·rupt′] *v.* **e·rupt·ing**

To break out with force, as lava does from a volcano: **The photographs of the volcano *erupting* in a fiery explosion were amazing.**

erupt

es·cape [i·skāp′] *v.* To get free or get away from danger: **The animals were able to *escape* from the forest fire. *syn.* flee**

Word Origins

escape What does taking off one's coat have to do with escaping? *Escape* comes from the Latin word *excappāre* first meaning "to take off one's cape or coat." By the time the word came into English, it meant "to throw off something that holds one back, or to gain one's freedom."

---

ex·pect [ik·spekt′] *v.* To be almost sure that something will happen; to consider something the right thing to do: **Mom and Dad *expect* us to make our beds every morning. *syn.* require**

ex·pres·sion [ik·spresh′ən] *n.* The tone of voice or look on the face that shows a person's feelings: **Tyrone's *expression* made it clear that he thought the joke was funny.**

fa·mil·iar [fə·mil′yər] *adj.* Well known from having been seen or heard many times: **The band played *familiar* tunes, and everyone sang along.**

Word Origins

familiar At first, *familiar* meant "of the family," from the Latin word *familiaris*. Its meaning grew to include friends and to become "known from being around often." *Familiar* began to be used in English in the 1300s.

---

fas·ten [fas′(ə)n] *v.* **fas·tened** To attach one thing to another: **Fred *fastened* the long tail to his mouse costume with a safety pin. *syn.* secure**

---

a add	e end	o odd	o͞o pool	oi oil	th this		a in *above*
ā ace	ē equal	ō open	u up	ou pout	zh vision		e in *sicken*
â care	i it	ô order	û burn	ng ring		ə =	i in *possible*
ä palm	ī ice	o͝o took	yo͞o fuse	th thin			o in *melon*
							u in *circus*

fault [fôlt] *n.* Guilt or responsibility for doing something wrong: **Juan said it was his *fault* that the dog got out, because he left the gate open.** *syn.* blame

firm [fûrm] *adj.* Not giving in: **Elena's teacher was *firm* about the rules in her class.** *syns.* unchanging; strict

fu·ri·ous·ly [fyŏŏr′ē•əs•lē] *adv.* With very strong effort: **Seth ran *furiously* toward the finish line, leaving the other runners far behind.**

glance [glans] *v.* **glanced** To look at very quickly: **Pete *glanced* at the sign on the door as he hurried past.**

guide [gīd] *v.* **guid·ed** To show someone the way to go: **The park ranger *guided* the lost hikers out of the woods.** *syn.* lead

gym [jim] *n.* (shortened form of *gymnasium*) A large room or building used for sports and for training athletes: **On Saturday mornings, basketball practice was held in the school *gym.***

har·mon·i·ca [här•mon′i•kə] *n.* A small musical instrument that a person blows into to make music: **Callie took the *harmonica* from her pocket and played a song.**

harmonica

ig·nore [ig•nôr′] *v.* To pay no attention to someone or something: **Never *ignore* traffic safety laws.**

Word Origins

ignore *Ignore* comes from the Latin word *ignorare*, which means "to not know" and so "to not pay attention to."

la·va [lä′və or lav′ə] *n.* Hot melted rock that pours out of the mouth of a volcano when it erupts: **When the volcano erupted, red-hot *lava* flowed down, covering the empty village.**

lava

lit·ter [lit′ər] *n.* Trash dropped on the ground and left there: **We filled trash bags with the paper cups and other *litter* people left along the parade route.**

lone·ly [lōn′lē] *adj.* The sad feeling caused by having no friends around or by missing someone: **I felt *lonely* when my friend Jason moved away.**

long [lông] *v.* **longed** To want to see someone or want something very much: **By the end of summer camp, Amy *longed* to see her family.** *syn.* desire

mag·net [mag′nit] *n.* **mag·nets** An object that can pull iron and steel towards it: **Colorful small *magnets* hold our drawings to the steel refrigerator door.**

ma·rine [mə·rēn′] *adj.* Having to do with the sea: **The scientist went scuba diving to collect *marine* plants for his research project.**

med·al [med′(ə)l] *n.* **med·als** An award given to winners in sports or other events: **Jena finished first in both contests and won two first-place *medals*.**

medals

mes·sage [mes′ij] *n.* Information passed on to a person by written words or by sound: **While we were out, Susan left a *message* on our telephone answering machine.**

me·ter [mē′tər] *n.* **me·ters** A basic measure of length in the metric system equal to about 39 inches or about 1 yard: **The length of the swimming pool was 50 *meters*, or about 55 yards.**

Fact File

metric system The metric system is a group of units used to make measurements. The base unit is the *meter*, and the other units get bigger and smaller by multiples of 10. Greek prefixes are used for units larger than the meter. *Kilo–* means 1,000, so a *kilometer* is 1,000 meters. Roman prefixes are used for units smaller than the meter. *Centi–* means 1/100, so a *centimeter* is 1/100 of a meter.

mus·tache [mus′tash *or* məs·tash′] *n.* The trimmed hair on a man's upper lip: **Grandpa's gray *mustache* curves down around the sides of his mouth.**

Word Origins

mustache *Mustache* came into English from the French in the 1500s. The French word came from the Italian *mostaccio*, which came from the Greek *mystax*, meaning "upper lip."

mustache

a add	e end	o odd	o͞o pool	oi oil	th this	a in *above*
ā ace	ē equal	ō open	u up	ou pout	zh vision	e in *sicken*
â care	i it	ô order	û burn	ng ring		ə = i in *possible*
ä palm	ī ice	o͝o took	yo͞o fuse	th thin		o in *melon*
						u in *circus*

367

no·tice [nō′tis] *v.* **no·ticed** To see something: **When Lee went to the animal shelter for a pet, he *noticed* two puppies curled up in a corner.** *syn.* observe

o·bey [ō·bā′] *v.* **o·beys** To do what one is told to do: **Our dog *obeys* all our orders, but our cat won't do anything we tell her to do.**

O·lym·pic Games [ō·lim′pik gāmz] *n.* An athletic contest held every four years in which athletes from all over the world take part: **My favorite event in the *Olympic Games* is diving, but I like to watch gymnastics, too.**

Fact File
Olympic Games Every four years the world's finest athletes compete in the many events of the Olympic Games. The first Olympic contest was held in 776 B.C. in the Stadium of Olympia in western Greece. There was only one event in the earliest contests. It was a footrace in which runners ran about 200 yards, or 180 meters.

om·e·let [om′lit or om′ə·lit] *n.* Eggs that have been beaten and cooked, sometimes with other foods: **The chef beat two eggs and added cheese and mushrooms as he cooked my *omelet.***

out·field·er [out′fēl′dər] *n.* A ballplayer who catches in the outfield, the area outside of the baseball diamond: **John's hit would have been a home run if the *outfielder* had not caught the ball.**

outfielder

pa·tient·ly [pā′shənt·lē] *adv.* Without fussing or complaining, even after a long time: **The child sat *patiently* for an hour until it was her turn to see the doctor.**

peace·ful [pēs′fəl] *adj.* Calm and quiet: **When the excitement of the parade was over, our street was *peaceful* once again.**

Word Origins
peaceful *Peace*, the base word of *peaceful*, comes from the Latin word *pax*, having a meaning similar to "fixed in place" or "safe." There are many English words that are related to *pax*, such as *pact*, *pacific*, and *pay*.

per·form [pər·fôrm′] *v.* To sing, dance, act, play a musical instrument, or use some other talent in front of an audience: **For the show, Leah will *perform* a song she wrote herself.**

perform

poi·son·ous [poi′zən·əs] *adj.* Describes a plant, animal, or product that sickens or kills living things by the use of a chemical: **A water moccasin is a *poisonous* snake whose bite can be deadly.** *syn.* toxic

prac·tice [prak′tis] *v.* **prac·ticed** To do something over and over to become better at it: **Tina *practiced* playing the piano for an hour every day.** *syn.* rehearse

pre·fer [pri·fûr′] *v.* To favor or choose one thing over another: **On warm, sunny days my sister and I *prefer* walking to school over taking the bus.**

pre·scrip·tion [pri·skrip′shən] *adj.* Having written instructions from a doctor: **Teresa had to take a *prescription* medicine to clear up her ear infection.**

pre·tend [pri·tend′] *v.* **pre·tend·ed** To make believe: **Diane did not want to answer her sister's questions, so she *pretended* to be asleep.**

pro·fes·sion·al [prə·fesh′ən·əl] *adj.* Describes people who are paid for what they do: **The New York Liberty is a women's *professional* basketball team.**

pro·gram [prō′gram′] *n.* Events or activities organized to help or teach others: **The city has a *program* that helps families find homes.** *syn.* plan

R

re·cite [ri·sīt′] *v.* To say something from memory: **He learned the poem by heart and is ready to *recite* it in front of the class.**

re·search [ri·sûrch′ *or* rē′sûrch′] *v.* **re·searched** To carefully check for facts by looking through reference sources: **Carmen *researched* her report about early flying machines by using encyclopedias and other books on that subject.**

re·spect [ri·spekt′] *v.* To treat someone politely; to admire someone because of what he or she has done: **Many classmates *respect* Carlos for studying so hard.**

re·spon·si·ble [ri·spon′sə·bəl] *adj.* Able to do what is needed on one's own: **Rosa is very *responsible* and will not forget to water your plants while you are away.** *syn.* reliable

S

se·ri·ous·ly [sir′ē·əs·lē] *adv.* In a thoughtful and honest way: **Brendan was always making jokes, so I was surprised when he spoke *seriously* about his poem.**

a	add	e	end	o	odd	o͞o	pool	oi	oil	th	this
ā	ace	ē	equal	ō	open	u	up	ou	pout	zh	vision
â	care	i	it	ô	order	û	burn	ng	ring		
ä	palm	ī	ice	o͝o	took	yo͞o	fuse	th	thin		

ə = {
a in *above*
e in *sicken*
i in *possible*
o in *melon*
u in *circus*
}

369

sort [sôrt] *v.* **sort·ing** To put similar objects into groups according to type, size, color, or other features: **Matthew was *sorting* through a box of keys, putting them in groups of small, medium, and large.**

splin·ter [splin′tər] *n.* **splin·ters** A very thin, sharp bit that breaks off a larger piece of wood, ice, metal, glass, or other material: **Wear shoes on the deck, or you might get *splinters* in your feet from the rough wood.**

splinters

sug·gest [sə(g)·jest′] *v.* **sug·gest·ed** To offer an idea in order to get others to do or think about something in a new or different way: **We had no plans for the afternoon, so Mia *suggested* that we go to the new aquarium.**

sur·vive [sər·vīv′] *v.* **sur·vived** To live through a difficult time: **The lost hiker *survived* the night on the snowy mountain and was rescued in the morning.** *syn.* outlast

tal·ent [tal′ənt] *n.* The ability to do something well, such as play a sport or a musical instrument: **With her *talent*, Gina is sure to be a famous artist one day.** *syn.* gift

tel·e·graph [tel′ə·graf′] *adj.* Having to do with messages sent and received through a machine by using electrical codes: **She went to the *telegraph* office to send her mother a birthday message.**

Fact File

telegraph The first useful telegraph machine was made by Samuel Morse in 1837. It used wires and electricity to send messages. Signals sent as long bursts of electricity were received at the other end as dashes. Signals sent as short bursts were received as dots. For example, the letter *e* is just one dot. This code is called Morse code.

tem·per·a·ture [tem′pər·ə·chər *or* tem′prə·chər] *n.* A measurement that tells in degrees how warm or cold something, such as the air, is: **The *temperature* at night was so low that one blanket wasn't enough to keep her warm.**

Word Origins

temperature At first *temperature* meant "mixture," such as "a temperature of brass and iron together." Later it was used to mean "mild weather," perhaps as a mixture of warm and cool air. The meaning used today probably came from this.

trail [trāl] *n.* A rough path through land where travel is difficult: **The forest *trail* had been made by settlers crossing the mountains.**

trail

train [trān] *v.* **trained** To teach people or animals to do something well by having them repeat the task over and over: **At batting practice, Mr. Lee *trained* us to keep our eyes on the ball.** *syn.* instruct

un·ex·pect·ed [un'ik•spek'tid] *adj.* Surprising; unplanned: **They were happy when their grandparents arrived for an *unexpected* visit.**

van·ish [van'ish] *v.* To go out of sight; to pass from sight: **The sun seemed to *vanish* when clouds covered the sky.** *syn.* disappear

Word Origins

vanish *Vanish* comes from the Latin word *evanescere*, meaning "to become empty," or "to disappear."

wise [wīz] *adj.* Able to understand why things happen in life as they do and to make good decisions based on that understanding: **The *wise* teacher listened to her students and helped them work out an agreement.**

a add	e end	o odd	o͞o pool	oi oil	t͟h this		a in *above*
ā ace	ē equal	ō open	u up	ou pout	zh vision		e in *sicken*
â care	i it	ô order	û burn	ng ring		ə =	i in *possible*
ä palm	ī ice	o͝o took	yo͞o fuse	th thin			o in *melon*
							u in *circus*

Page numbers in color refer to biographical information.

Acknowledgments

For permission to reprint copyrighted material, grateful acknowledgment is made to the following sources:

Boyds Mills Press, Inc.: "To" and cover from *Been to Yesterdays* by Lee Bennett Hopkins. Text and cover copyright © 1995 by Lee Bennett Hopkins.

Candlewick Press, Cambridge, MA: "The Talent Show" from *Don't Call Me Beanhead!* by Susan Wojciechowski, cover illustration by Susanna Natti. Text copyright © 1994 by Susan Wojciechowski; cover illustration copyright © 1994 by Susanna Natti.

Children's Television Workshop, New York, NY: From "A Place of Their Own" by Carol Pugliano in *Contact Kids* Magazine, March 1998. Text copyright 1998 by Children's Television Workshop.

Clarion Books/Houghton Mifflin Company: *Rosie: A Visiting Dog's Story* by Stephanie Calmenson, photographs by Justin Sutcliffe. Text copyright © 1994 by Stephanie Calmenson; photographs copyright © 1994 by Justin Sutcliffe.

Crown Publishers, Inc.: Cover illustration by Nancy Carpenter from *Lester's Dog* by Karen Hesse. Illustration copyright © 1993 by Nancy Carpenter.

Tui De Roy: From "Wild Shots, They're My Life" by Tui De Roy in *Ranger Rick* Magazine, August 1996.

Dial Books for Young Readers, a division of Penguin Putnam Inc.: Cover illustration by Jerry Pinkney from *Back Home* by Gloria Jean Pinkney. Illustration copyright © 1992 by Jerry Pinkney.

Farrar, Straus & Giroux, Inc.: *Turtle Bay* by Saviour Pirotta, illustrated by Nilesh Mistry. Text copyright © 1997 by Saviour Pirotta; illustrations copyright © 1997 by Nilesh Mistry.

Charles Ghigna: "Dream Boat" by Charles Ghigna from *Ranger Rick* Magazine, June 1998. Text copyright 1998 by Charles Ghigna.

Grosset & Dunlap, Inc., a division of Penguin Putnam Inc.: "Water Woman" by S. A. Kramer from *Wonder Women of Sports*, cover illustration by Mitchell Heinze. Text copyright © 1997 by S. A. Kramer; cover illustration © 1997 by Mitchell Heinze.

Harcourt, Inc.: Text and cover illustration from *The Science Book of Magnets* by Neil Ardley. Copyright © 1991 by Neil Ardley; cover illustration copyright © 1991 by Dorling Kindersley Limited. Cover illustration from *Seal Surfer* by Michael Foreman. Copyright © 1996 by Michael Foreman. Cover illustration by Scott Medlock from *Opening Days: Sports Poems*, selected by Lee Bennett Hopkins. Illustration copyright © 1996 by Scott Medlock. Cover illustration from *Frida María* by Deborah Nourse Lattimore. Copyright © 1994 by Deborah Nourse Lattimore.

Highlights for Children, Inc., Columbus, OH: "The Last Case of the I.C. Detective Agency" by Carol M. Harris and cover illustration by Cheryl Kirk Noll from *Highlights for Children* Magazine, January 1996. Text and cover illustration copyright © 1996 by Highlights for Children, Inc.

Holiday House, Inc.: *Little Grunt and the Big Egg* by Tomie dePaola. Copyright © 1990 by Tomie dePaola.

Alfred A. Knopf, Inc.: Cover illustration by Raul Colón from *Tomás and the Library Lady* by Pat Mora. Illustration copyright © 1997 by Raul Colón.

Lee & Low Books Inc., 95 Madison Ave., New York, NY 10016: *Allie's Basketball Dream* by Barbara E. Barber, illustrated by Darryl Ligasan. Text copyright © 1996 by Barbara E. Barber; illustrations copyright © 1996 by Darryl Ligasan.

Little, Brown and Company: *Arthur Writes a Story* by Marc Brown. Copyright © 1996 by Marc Brown. Cover illustration from *Arthur's New Puppy* by Marc Brown. Copyright © 1993 by Marc Brown. Cover illustration from *Arthur's Pet Business* by Marc Brown. Copyright © 1990 by Marc Brown. From *Centerfield Ballhawk* by Matt Christopher, cover illustration by Ellen Beier. Text copyright © 1992 by Matthew F. Christopher; cover illustration copyright © 1992 by Ellen Beier.

Lothrop, Lee & Shepard Books, a division of William Morrow & Company, Inc.: Cover illustration by Alan Tiegreen from *Ramona Quimby, Age 8* by Beverly Cleary. Copyright © 1981 by Beverly Cleary.

Macmillan Library Reference: *Marta's Magnets* by Wendy Pfeffer, illustrated by Gail Piazza. Text © 1995 by Wendy Pfeffer; illustrations © 1995 by Gail Piazza.

Margaret K. McElderry Books, an imprint of Simon & Schuster Children's Publishing Division: "The Swimmer" from *A Tree Place and Other Poems* by Constance Levy. Text copyright © 1994 by Constance Kling Levy.

The Millbrook Press: Cover illustration by Christopher O'Neill and cover photograph by Roger Vlitos from *How do I feel about: Making Friends* by Sarah Levete. © 1996 by Aladdin Books Ltd; U.S. text © 1998.

Morrow Junior Books, a division of William Morrow & Company, Inc.: From *Ramona Forever* by Beverly Cleary, cover illustration by Alan Tiegreen. Text copyright © 1984 by Beverly Cleary; cover illustration copyright © 1984 by William Morrow & Company, Inc.

Pantheon Books, a division of Random House, Inc.: From *The Stories Julian Tells* by Ann Cameron, cover illustration by Ann Strugnell. Text copyright © 1981 by Ann Cameron; cover illustration copyright © 1981 by Ann Strugnell.

Philomel Books, a division of Penguin Putnam Inc.: Cover illustration from *Appelemando's Dreams* by Patricia Polacco. Copyright © 1991 by Patricia Polacco.

G. P. Putnam's Sons, a division of Penguin Putnam Inc.: *Officer Buckle and Gloria* by Peggy Rathmann. Copyright © 1995 by Peggy Rathmann.

Random House, Inc.: Cover illustration by Dora Leder from *Julian's Glorious Summer* by Ann Cameron. Illustration copyright © 1987 by Dora Leder.

Scholastic Inc.: Cover illustration by Varnette P. Honeywood from *The Treasure Hunt* by Bill Cosby. Copyright © 1997 by Bill Cosby. CARTWHEEL BOOKS and the CARTWHEEL BOOKS logo are trademarks and/or registered trademarks of Scholastic Inc. "Balto, the Dog Who Saved Nome" from *Seven True Dog Stories* by Margaret Davidson, cover illustration by Susanne Suba. Copyright © 1977 by Margaret Davidson. Cover illustration from *Ibis: A True Whale Story* by John Himmelman. Copyright © 1990 by John Himmelman. Cover photograph from *My Horse of the North* by Bruce McMillan. Copyright © 1997 by Bruce McMillan. Cover illustration from *Ruby the Copycat* by Peggy Rathmann. Copyright © 1991 by Margaret Rathmann.

Simon & Schuster Books for Young Readers, an imprint of Simon & Schuster Children's Publishing Division: Cover illustration by Nancy Winslow Parker from *The Goat in the Rug* by Charles L. Blood and Martin Link. Illustration copyright © 1976 by Nancy Winslow Parker. Cover illustration by Paul Yalowitz from *Nell Nugget and the Cow Caper* by Judith Ross Enderle and Stephanie Gordon Tessler. Illustration copyright © 1996 by Paul Yalowitz. "All My Hats" from *Secrets of a Small Brother* by Richard J. Margolis, cover illustration by Donald Carrick. Text copyright © 1984 by Richard J. Margolis; cover illustration copyright © 1984 by Donald Carrick.

Steck-Vaughn Company: From *Baseball: How To Play the All-Star Way* (Retitled: "Spotlight On Baseball") by Mark Alan Teirstein. Text copyright © 1994 by Steck-Vaughn Company.

Viking Penguin, a division of Penguin Putnam Inc.: Cover illustration by Wayne Alfano from *The Math Wiz* by Betsy Duffey. Illustration copyright © 1992 by Wayne Alfano. *Ronald Morgan Goes to Camp* by Patricia Reilly Giff, illustrated by Susanna Natti. Text copyright © 1995 by Patricia Reilly Giff; illustrations copyright © 1995 by Susanna Natti.

Photo Credits

Key: (t)=top, (b)=bottom, (c)=center, (l)=left, (r)=right

Pete Saloutos/The Stock Market, 109; David Madison, 114-115; Pete Saloutos/The Stock Market, 116-117; Pete Saloutos/The Stock Market, 122-123; Tui de Roy/ Roving Tortoise, 180-191; UPI/Corbis-Bettmann, 194, 198, 206, 208, 213 ; © 1998 Suki Coughlin/Paula McFarland, stylist, 233; J. Gerard Smith, 234-235; Justin Sutcliffe, 286-305; courtesy, Matt Christopher, 325(t); Margaret Miller, 353; Jim Steinberg/Tony Stone Images, 364; Gail Shumway/FPG, 366(l); Inge Spence/Tom Stack & Associates, 367; Richard Johnston/Tony Stone Images, 368; Ron Thomas /FPG, 369(l); Joyce Photographics/Photo Researchers, 369(r); John D. Cunningham/Visuals Unlimited, 371(l); Bob Krist/The Stock Market, 371(r).

All other photos by Harcourt, Inc.:

Rick Friedman/Black Star, Lisa Quinones/Black Star, Tom Sobolik/Black Star, Walt Chrynwski/Black Star, George Robinson/Black Star, John Troha/Black Star, Sal diMarco/Black Star, Nancy Pierce/Black Star, Dale Higgins.

Illustration Credits

Jon Goodell, Cover Art; Tungwai Chau, 2-3, 10-11, 12-13, 124-125; Tracy Sabin, 4-5, 126-127, 128-129, 238-239; Cindy Lindgren, 6-7, 240-241, 242-243, 358-359; Marc Brown, 14-35, 36-37; Gail Piazza, 40-59, 62-63; Susanna Natti, 64-79, 80-81; Darryl Ligasan, 84-103, 106-107; Mark Bender, 104-105; Kurt Nagahori, 120-121; Peggy Rathmann, 130-151, 152-153; Nilesh Mistry, 156-175, 178-179; Dave Calver, 176-177; Doug Rugh, 194-209, 212-213; Tomie dePaola, 214-233, 236-237; Cornelius Van Wright & Ying Hwa Hu, 244-259, 260-261; Laura Ovresat, 264-279, 284-285; Linda Helton, 280-283; Larry Johnson, 308-325, 326-327, 328-329; Diane Greenseid, 330-353, 356-357; Robert Casilla, 354-355; Klaus Heesch, 109,120; Ethan Long, 176,331; Mike DiGiorgio, 326; Vilma Ortiz-Dillon, 210-211; Dave Herrick, 38-39; Catharine Bennett, 82-83, 262-263; Katy Farmer, 54-155; Billy Davis, 192-193